Homiletic Meditations Cycle B

Pentecost Through The Feast Of Christ The King

Gospel
The Spirit's Tether
By Leonard H. Budd

* * *

Gospel
Assayings: Theological Faith Testings
By Robert L. Salzgeber

* * *

Gospel
Spectators Or Sentinels?
By Arthur H. Kolsti

CSS Publishing Company, Inc.
Lima, Ohio

HOMILETIC MEDITATIONS — CYCLE B
THE SPIRIT'S TETHER
ASSAYINGS: THEOLOGICAL FAITH TESTINGS
SPECTATORS OR SENTINELS?

Copyright © 1993 by
The CSS Publishing Company, Inc.
Lima, Ohio

All rights reserved. No part of this publication may be reproduced, stored in a retrieval system, or transmitted in any form or by any means, electronic, mechanical, photocopying, recording, or otherwise, without the prior permission of the publisher. Inquiries should be addressed to: The CSS Publishing Company, Inc., 628 South Main Street, Lima, Ohio 45804.

Scripture quotations are from the *New Revised Standard Version of the Bible*, copyright 1989 by the Division of Christian Education of the National Council of the Churches of Christ in the USA, and the *Revised Standard Version of the Bible*, copyrighted 1946, 1952, (c), 1971, 1973, by the Division of Christian Education of the National Council of the Churches of Christ in the USA. Used by permission.

Library of Congress Cataloging-in-Publication Data

Budd, Leonard H., 1933-
   The Spirit's tether : sermons for Pentecost (first third) gospel, cycle B / by Leonard H. Budd.
     p.   cm.
   ISBN 1-55673-608-8
   1. Pentecost season — Sermons. 2. Sermons, American. 3. Bible. N.T. Gospels — Sermons. I. Title.
   BV61.B84   1993
252'.6—dc20
                                                              93-2757
                                                                  CIP

Library of Congress Cataloging-in-Publication Data

Salzgeber, Robert L., 1947-
   Assayings : theological faith testings : sermons for Pentecost (Middle Third) gospel / by Robert L. Salzgeber.
     p.   cm. — (Cycle B gospel texts)
   ISBN 1-55673-609-6
   1. Church year sermons. 2. Bible. N.T. Gospels — Sermons. 3. Common lectionary. 4. Lectionary preaching. I. Title. II. Series.
   BV4253.S32   1993
252'.6—dc20
                                                              93-18002
                                                                    CIP

Library of Congress Cataloging-in-Publication Data

Kolsti, Arthur, 1925-
   Spectators or sentinels? : sermons for Pentecost (last third) gospel, cycle B / by Arthur H. Kolsti.
     p.   cm.
   ISBN 1-55673-610-X
   1. Pentecost season — Sermons. 2. Sermons, American. 3. Bible. N.T. Gospels — Sermons. I. Title.
   BV61.K65   1993
252'.6—dc20
                                                              92-2758
                                                                    CIP

9363 / ISBN 1-55673-639-8

Table Of Contents — Gospel

The Spirit's Tether

Introduction — 9

Pentecost Sunday — 15
God's Descending Spirit
John 20:19-23

Trinity Sunday — 21
Our Own Mountaintop Walk
Matthew 28:16-20

Corpus Christi — 27
It's A Small World After All
Mark 14:12-16; 22-26

Ordinary Time 9 — 33
The M And M Factor
Mark 2:23—3:6

Ordinary Time 10 — 39
Have You Confronted Christ?
Mark 3:20-35

Ordinary Time 11 — 45
Pathway To God's Kingdom
Mark 4:26-34

Ordinary Time 12 — 51
Walking Through A Storm
Mark 4:35-41

Ordinary Time 13   57
    Living By Faith And Trust
    Mark 5:21-43

Ordinary Time 14   63
    Walking The Familiar
    Mark 6:1-6

Ordinary Time 15   71
    A Solitary Witness
    Mark 6:7-13

Ordinary Time 16   77
    The Compassionate Highway
    Mark 6:30-34

Table Of Contents — Gospel

Assayings: Theological Faith Testings

Ordinary Time 17   85
Sarah And The WECON Council
John 6:1-5

Ordinary Time 18   93
Charlie Used To Do That
John 6:24-35

Ordinary Time 19   99
The Robe
John 6:41-51

Ordinary Time 20   105
The Banquet
John 6:51-58

Ordinary Time 21   111
Gunda
John 6:60-69

Ordinary Time 22   119
Changing The Rules
Mark 7:1-8, 14-15, 21-23

Ordinary Time 23   125
The Spiritual Organ of Corti
Mark 7:31-37

Ordinary Time   131
God's Math: Lose Life = Save It
Mark 8:27-35

Ordinary Time 25 137
  A Formula For Greatness
  Mark 9:30-37

Ordinary Time 26 143
  *When Is It Tolerable To Be Intolerant?
  Mark 9:38-43, 45, 47-48

Ordinary Time 27 147
  Learning The Basics
  Mark 10:2-16

*This homily is by Donald Macleod. It was originally published in *Know The Way, Keep The Truth, Win The Life,* (CSS 7858).

Table Of Contents — Gospel

Spectators Or Sentinels?

Ordinary Time 28   155
The Running Man
Mark 10:17-30

Ordinary Time 29   161
No Short Cuts To Glory
Mark 10:35-45

Ordinary Time 30   167
Seeing And Not Seeing
Mark 10:46-52

Ordinary Time 31   173
Less Important Does Not Mean Unimportant
Mark 12:28-34

Ordinary Time 32   179
Dwarfed By Comparison
Mark 12:38-44

Ordinary Time 33   185
Spectators Or Sentinels?
Mark 13:24-32

All Saints' Sunday   191
It's Time To Rediscover The Beatitudes
Matthew 5:1-12

Christ The King   197
Where Do We Stand?
John 18:33-37

Thanksgiving Day   201
Good Powers Wonderfully Hidden
Matthew 6:25-33

The Spirit's Tether

Leonard H. Budd

Introduction

As the sun broke over the edge of the city wall it brought warmth back to the little doorways where old men sat. The sun's heat, in its first brush after the cold night, made steam rise from the flat, stone surfaces. Jerusalem, set upon the high mountain, captured the cold of night so that windows were shuttered and the heaviest cloaks were wrapped tight. But with a new day's sun upon the stone, the city warmed. Windows opened. Doors were tethered open. Humanity moved outside to begin the business of another day.

Only this day the sun announced the Pentecost holiday. Visitors from distant lands now filled the streets. They crowded the marketplaces, bartering for food. Wise merchants knew the coin of every realm. They were not outbid by foreign traders. On this Pentecost the market square was filled. Even the doorways were crowded and the din of human voices was matched by the braying of animals, the barking of dogs, the scraping of heavy boxes upon the worn stone walks.

The entrance to the square held the well. It provided the only water for that part of Jerusalem. A young man stood by the wood frame staring long and hard upon the crowds. It appeared from his dress that he was from Galilee — the rough, peasant Galilee. It was not hard to guess that this was his first visit to the Holy City.

Nearby two older men were talking. One was balding and fat. The other was heavily bearded and highly animated in his talking. They seemed detached from the crowds. So intent were they in their conversation that a boy walking with a donkey almost knocked down the bearded man but the man did not stop his talk nor his waving arms.

A mother and child come out of a doorway, the child still rubbing sleep from his eyes. Quickly they crossed the square, moving directly to the well. Once there they drew water and returned as quickly to their home. They did not speak to anyone, nor to each other.

From the temple end of the square a royal, robed priest moved through the crowd. Actually the crowd separated so that he had a clear path. He, too, did not speak to anyone. His step had a haughty gait, as if he really did not want to be so close to so many common people.

And there were many others in the square that morning so that the whole square was like a churning pool of water, forever moving, currents forever flowing, in an ebb and flow of humanity.

As one surveyed the noisy, international crowd and looked to all the buildings that framed the square, one structure remained shuttered to the warmth of that new day. Only one. Its two windows were covered with wood planks, fastened to the inside. The door, marked with mud at its base, was closed. It was a door with no outside handle. Once closed and locked within it would remain shut tight. And it remained so all morning.

Then, very suddenly, the closed door burst open. Men were running out of the room, out into the busy, surging square. Some immediately began talking, shouting to those nearby. Others ran toward the well, to the high ledge that marked that part of the square. The one with the loudest voice, and the largest frame, shouted for quiet. Then he told of Jesus, his Lord and Master! And people who you would think could not understand did understand. It was a miracle. It was the birth of the church.

The event of the Christian Pentecost as recorded in the first chapters of Acts describes one way by which God's Holy Spirit took hold of human lives and worked transformation. Scriptures of this Pentecost Season tell additional stories of the Spirit's work, inviting us into that "journey of the spirit."

Each chapter is introduced by an imagined scene. "It might have been this way." These little stories may be used within the sermon or as an introduction by another reader. Perhaps they might be used as a drama, complete with costume. They seek to set the scene for the scripture and sermon.

These chapters are dedicated to one who has shared not only the spiritual journey but the earthly one as well — to my wife, Karen. Through her own study of scripture and through her own professional work in the field of nursing research, she has been both inspiration and companion. My love and admiration — and a sense of the Holy Spirit's guidance and protection — marks this dedication.

— Leonard H. Budd
Cleveland, Ohio
September, 1992

Pentecost Sunday
John 20:19-23

God's Descending Spirit

Even in the room's darkness Rachel's face was seen streaked with tears. She wiped her cheeks with the back of her hand. Rachel had been an un-named disciple since Jesus had first visited her village. They had already celebrated two passovers. It had been that long ago. She was not important in the way that Simon and his brothers were important. She could not speak eloquently, nor command evil spirits to disappear. Nor could she carry her side of debate about the religious law. Also, she was a woman. But Rachel called Jesus her Lord. She considered herself a disciple and traveled with that loyal band up to the Holy City. That meant that she had been in the temple crowd when Jesus debated the rulers. She had been in the shadows of the upper room and in the darkness of the garden. She shared in the horror of crucifixion hill — and in the empty loss the day after. It was just too much for her to accept. "How could God do this," she sobbed.

Now, in the dusk of the first day of a new week she, and the other better known disciples, were learning that God was using even the shameful cross for his purpose. She was learning that by the power of the Spirit-presence there was yet work to do. Rachel's tears of deep grief were becoming others tears — in time, tears of joy.

Back during a time when boys were drafted into the armed service, a devout young man was drafted from a farm in south Georgia and was sent into the army. He had never been but a few miles from his home. Now he was suddenly thrust into a new, highly structured environment. But as he left his home he took with him the Christian faith and practices that had been an important part of his life since childhood. That meant, for him, such things as reading the Bible regularly and kneeling by his bed each night for a time of prayer.

Such overt piety infuriated the rough sergeant who was in charge of the company of recruits. He set about to deliberately humiliate the young Christian. He sought to make the young man's life over into the image of hostility and brute force that he (the sergeant) lived. That sergeant abused the man verbally. He issued him all sorts of unfair treatment. He used every opportunity to harass the soldier. Yet, at no point did the young Georgian resort to "returning evil for evil." He endured all the abuse without a word of complaint. Again and again he found occasion to do kind things for his antagonist.

Late one Saturday night the sergeant came through the barracks three-fourths drunk. On seeing the young man kneeling by his bunk, the sergeant exploded. He shouted, and tried every way he could to distract the boy. When nothing seemed to work, the sergeant took off one of his muddy, heavy boots and threw it at the boy. Sailing across the room it hit the young man on the back of the head. It stunned him so that he fell to the floor. In a moment he regained his composure and without a word resumed his prayer time by the side of his bunk. Further enraged, the sergeant took off the other boot and flung it at the young recruit. It, too, hit the boy, but he did not retaliate in anger. Then the sergeant reeled off a string of oaths and stumbled into his own quarters and to bed.

The next morning when the sergeant awoke with swollen eyes and throbbing head, the first thing he saw were his boots: clean and polished, sitting by his bed. The sight was more than he could take. With tears in his eyes he walked into the barracks, found the young man and said, "What is it with you?

I have done everything in my power to break you. Instead, you have broken me. What do you know that I do not know? What is your secret? What is your power?"

The young boy replied, "God's Spirit!"

That is a story from which afternoon soap operas are made — or used to be made. At its most profound level it is witness to the sensed presence of God in life. That young recruit was giving witness to the unseen things that mattered in his life, spiritual affirmations. He was living out a belief that God is a very real presence in daily life. That witness is the singular purpose of this homily!

To be such a person, as the Bible defines it, is to be a person touched by God's Holy Spirit. God's Holy Spirit: that mysterious influence that takes human life, buoys it up to heights beyond which it otherwise could not attain. The Holy Spirit: gifting strength when we are prone to weakness. The Holy Spirit: offering moral guidance when we tend to drift. The Holy Spirit: providing courage and trust when we are apt to be afraid and cynical. One writer says, "The Holy Spirit is the NOW-NESS of God." It is the immediate presence, the power of God in the moment. It certainly was for that young recruit.

The scripture text is of a remembrance from Easter evening. In fear the disciples are hiding. In that dark fear, Christ "stood among them." In his presence they are confronted with the peace and power of that Holy Spirit. In a way it can be understood as the transfer of that peace and power that began for Jesus down by the Dead Sea. It was the beginning of his earthly ministry.

Jesus was 30 years old, we suspect. He encountered his cousin, John, in that hot, scrubby, separated, devastated area. John was preaching a call to repentance, inviting people to a change in life. He was marking that interior change with a sacramental washing in the Jordan waters. People came from all over the territory to hear the preacher, and to receive the baptism.

John spoke of the evil that lurks in the hearts of men and women. He spoke of the great calamities that awaited those who did not repent of their evil and return to God's ways. His use of the Jordan waters was a symbol for washing away the past evil, washing away the past lethargy, washing away the past sin! And the crowds responded. They came to him as in an ancient Woodstock! They plunged into the Jordan to have their spirits washed clean. They stepped up on the river's shore newly washed in God's sight!

But John was familiar with the ancient expectations of the people. He knew of the coming Messiah! And he knew that Messiah would not only cleanse, he would also liberate the people — set them free to be what God intended. Messiah would offer a new relationship to God. John saw himself as preparing the way for that Messiah. Into the muddy waters of the Jordan stepped the carpenter from Nazareth. Some accounts of scripture say that John saw him, singled him out. (Matthew, John) In other reports, Jesus is simply part of the crowds that sought baptism in the river's water. (Mark, Luke)

In either case, Jesus was alone in those moments. That is usually the situation, isn't it? Life's biggest moments come internally — inside us, working in such ways that the world outside is unaware! He was there gifted with the Holy Spirit of God. He entered the water as Jesus from Nazareth. He left the river as Jesus the Christ, the anointed One.

But, of course, there is more to the mystery of God's spirit. What became a presence for Jesus was promised to those who followed him. Now that Jesus' earthly ministry is ended, that Spirit is handed on to those who must continue the ministry. John's gospel — in this text — tells of this spiritual baptism being given the frightened disciples the very evening of the Easter affirmation. Other scriptures tell of this gift coming later. "Wait," said Jesus in Luke's remembrance, "Wait for the gift of God's spirit." (Acts 1:4)

And it did come! With that gift the disciples became apostles. The Holy Spirit changed them from learners to teachers, from receivers to givers. And it has continued through the ages, right down to the current moment. It is a gift to you! Life today finds strength and meaning in that Holy Spirit of God.

Do you remember Paul's words, speaking to Christians in Corinth? "In each of us the Spirit is manifested in one particular way, for some useful purpose. One, through the spirit, has the gift of wise speech, while another, by the power of the same spirit, can put the deepest knowledge into words. Another, by the same spirit, is granted faith; another, by the one spirit, gifts of healing and other miraculous powers, another has the gift of prophecy, and another the ability to distinguish true spirits from false, yet another has the gift of ecstatic utterance of different kinds and another the ability to interpret it. But all these gifts are the work of one and the same spirit." (1 Corinthians 12:7-11)

I am not old enough and, I hope, am honest enough, never to presume to say how God's Holy Spirit works. That is mystery. My mortalness is too real to pronounce the Spirit's limits, where its presence is most seen, best seen or not seen. I really cannot preach of where the spirit of God touches you! I do believe that the boy who confronted his army sergeant knew the "nowness" of God for his life. He had received the Holy Spirit in an enduring and empowering way. But that is one boy in one situation.

The witness of the church is that God's Holy Spirit, coming down upon a receptive humanity, works miracles!

John Wesley changed a nation's understanding of the work of God's spirit as he moved across England 250 years ago. He was the little man who found "my heart strangely warmed" by God's Holy Spirit. The Wesleyan openness to the leading of God gave birth to many a human transformation. Two hundred fifty years ago John Wesley, touched by God's Spirit, worked miracles!

And, I believe that about Mother Teresa today. We remember her gentle touch upon the untouchables, upon those persons who would have had only the street curb upon which to die, except for her kindness, her divine caring. God's Holy Spirit came into her life in such ways that community life was sensitized to a great human need. All people of good will see the presence of God's Holy Spirit through her living.

But it is not just for the historic or famous. You and I know that God's spirit has been part of the lives of some good folks whom we have known and continue to know. We thank God for them! There are countless examples of God's spirit within daily life. God's Holy Spirit is reality!

Therefore, the only conclusion to this witness is to call us to be open to the Spirit's leading — to be open to God's descending presence. The only purpose of this preaching is to encourage each of us to move into living in such ways that we may receive and hold that Spirit — to encounter the experiences of living in such ways, with such open-mindedness, that the Holy Spirit may be received. Such is the promise and the power!

Trinity Sunday
Matthew 28:16-20

Our Own Mountaintop Walk

Matthias was the 13th of the 12 disciples! He had been chosen by lot to fill the 12th spot when Judas had removed himself from the close circle of Jesus' followers. Matthias had followed the crowds down from the Galilee and had been close to all the disciples through much of the teaching years. And so, with the casting of the lots that picked him, Matthias joined the inner circle of disciples.

He was a serious man, trained in the religious law, and certain that Jesus was the expected Messiah. So certain was he that he had literally left his family — they had disowned him! His certainty was affirmed by the words of holy writing that he knew so well, and by the words that he had heard from Jesus' lips and the deeds accomplished by Jesus' touch. "This is our Messiah," he often said. "This is the Lord."

The one regret that burned in his heart was that he was not with the 11 when Jesus, radiant, had appeared to the disciples for a last earthly time. He quizzed the other disciples often. "What did Jesus say on the mountain?" "What did he look like?" "How did he seem to you?" "Was he with you for a long time?" And, most important, "Tell me about his words." The 11 would recount it all, ending with Jesus' direction to "Go to all peoples."

That was exactly what Matthias planned to do! He would do what Jesus had said, even though he had not heard the Lord's voice speak. He would leave the Galilee, he would travel across Judea down to the Sea and he would take a ship to some far place. There he would speak about Jesus the Messiah. He would do what Jesus had asked for he was now one of the 12.

Although it is not known with certainty, tradition says that Matthias was beheaded for his missionary work in Judea.

"In Fourteen Hundred and Ninety-two Columbus sailed the ocean blue!" Recently the world marked the 500th anniversary of Christopher Columbus' adventure in the Santa Maria. As we all now know, he did not end up where he was headed, which is why some native Americans are now called Indians. He did not "discover" a new world because others before him knew of it — some even lived upon it! He did make a lasting connection between the two continents, but his legacy to the populations he visited was not necessarily a blessing. This man from Genoa believed "God granted me the gift of knowledge ... (and) revealed to me that it was feasible to sail ... to the Indies, and placed in me a burning desire to carry out this plan." Columbus set out with a belief that he had tested with his mind, and with a faith to which he was willing to give his life! How many of us can walk in Columbus' shoes? When, on Friday, August 3, 1492, the "Nina, the Pinta, and the Santa Maria," eased away from their moorings at Palos, in southern Spain, Columbus was putting his beliefs and his faith into the realities of life.

Before the reports of his trans-Atlantic travel penetrated the Old World, Spanish coins had stamped upon them an outline of the Straits of Gibraltar. Underneath the outline of the Straits was the Latin inscription *Ne Plus Ultra*. It translates, "No more beyond." It meant that the world ended in the great expansive voids of water beyond the Straits. There was nothing more. But once Columbus returned home and told of what he had seen, of what he had discovered, and once that report was widely shared, then new coins were minted. The inscription was changed to *Plus Ultra*. It translates, "More beyond!"

That is the mountaintop affirmation which came to the disciples in Galilee and the word that ends Matthew's gospel. And those 11 disciples — and we who follow in their footsteps — claim the authority to speak that message to the world! What had been a wall, a great confinement, is now the arch of a great doorway, an entry! It is an entry into much that gives us joy!

Part of the joy is knowledge that the harsh limits of brutality, fear, hate and force are not the ultimate boundaries of human life.

In Jesus' century, no death was more tortuous, brutal, demeaning than that of hanging naked upon a wooden cross and publicly dying of thirst and hunger and sheer exposure. It was cruel. To the Jew it was shameful. It was meant to break every possible quality of human will, and in the end to break the physical body as that last breath was expelled, or that last drop of blood issued. The possibility of crucifixion hung over the head of every human life in that Roman world.

But the reports that emerged out of the first Easter told the amazing, mind-altering story that this perfect machine of death did not end life! The Jesus who had walked through the Garden of Gethsemane now walked in Joseph's garden! The Jesus who taught upon a hillside still taught. His words were vivid and direct — and still life-changing. The power of that resurrection reality for the disciples turned everything around. Life's deep, dark valley was instead a mountaintop!

The great defeat that Roman soldiers were so sure would silence the Nazarene did not end his life. Those who made that discovery shouted that God's power is greater than the world's power! Their shout is now our shout.

There is a beautiful poem that marks this affirmation. It is one of my favorites, and one that has ministered to my life. Edwin Markham wrote:

> *Defeat may serve as well as victory*
> *To shake the soul and let the glory out.*
> *When the great oak is straining in the wind,*

> *The boughs drink in new beauty, and the trunk*
> *Sends down a deeper root on the windward side.*
> *Only the soul that knows the mighty grief*
> *Can know the mighty rapture. Sorrows come*
> *To stretch out spaces in the heart for joy.*

There could not have been a greater grief, nor defeat, than that borne by the disciples as the dark shadows of crucifixion Friday fell upon the beginning week. Every hope they had shared was broken. Every dream they dreamed was shattered. The kingdom that their Lord had introduced was now encased in frightened and hiding Galileans. Peter now knew that even their upcountry accents could get them in trouble. The windows were shuttered. The door was locked from the inside. But then, the discovery was made, "Defeat may serve as well as victory to shake the soul and let the glory out." Defeat became the victory!

In wondrous ways that discovery translates into our living, doesn't it?

The discovery is affirmed in the acts of forgiveness expressed within families that now allow for the joy of family love to be regained.

It is affirmed in the acts of charity and caring that are offered across all sorts of worldly boundaries, and the "walls come tumbling down." As illustration, it is in Bread for the World, a Christian organization seeking to feed the hungry. They report that one of every five children in the world are "at risk of hunger." The affirmation of Easter is in their work, seeking to turn death into life for millions of children in the world.

It is affirmed in the great variety of people and ideas who can come together in one congregation — this one — to study in many church school classes and to work together in deeds of charity. This is all done in Christ, as part of the body of the Risen Lord.

The Spanish coin said *Plus Ultra*. "More beyond." Easter's translation of hope in this world is that God's forces of love are greater than the forces of hate and violence. Christians live in that affirmation.

The Spirit presence of Christ is also an affirmation that the great finality of earth's death is not boundary of the human spirit. "More beyond." The enemy, death, is defeated. "Death where is thy sting," wrote Paul. Christians share that belief. It is belief in something yet unproven, as with Columbus' venture from the port of Palos. It is belief in life eternal, living no longer tied to matters of earth, life no longer limited by a body's breath or a heart's beat. The enemy had always been death. Now, in the resurrection faith, there is more beyond! It remains a mystery, but it is held in the power of faith. And in that faith there is no defeat that can overpower the victory.

Some time ago I read a fascinating story. It may only be a story. It is told, not to articulate history but to underscore the victory faith! Wellington and Napoleon were fighting the battle of Waterloo. It was a decisive battle. Life for many, many persons hinged on its outcome. At last, word was transmitted to London by means of semaphores — a visual code with reflected sunlight spelling out the message letter by letter. A sentry picked up the message from his post atop a great cathedral. Letter by letter he passed on the message to London. The first word was "Wellington." The second word was "defeated."

Suddenly a very dense fog settled in upon the cathedral, making it impossible for the light to penetrate the mists and allow the message forwarded on. The fog grew more dense, and its darkness was mirrored in the hearts of the Londoners who had received the word, "Wellington defeated." It meant that Napoleon had won. The English of London were a conquered people. Hope was gone. Liberty was no more. England was ruled by another.

But as suddenly as it had come, the fog lifted. The sentry returned to his tower, and went back to his duties, feverishly attempting to transmit the whole message. And London saw it — the good news breaking upon the city and telling the full story: "Wellington defeated the enemy!"

Whether the semaphores' message to London is history or fiction, it does convey the truth of Christian faith! That truth is the shout first heard in Joseph's garden as the earliest followers of Christ made the discovery. It is the victory message of Jesus' word to his disciples upon that Galilee mountaintop, and it is the shout heard through the centuries as human life has been understood as life lived in two worlds — one temporal, the other eternal. Even *Newsweek* magazine lists deaths under the heading of "Transition."

It is the victory word uttered by you and others who sense that God's gift of Jesus Christ is to redeem life from death. It is the victory word shared in Jesus' last word to his disciples. After the Easter resurrection, the 11 return to Galilee and to a retreat that was known to all of them — a mountaintop retreat. Jesus is with them. They understand his authority over them, over all the life that God has given. His word is both a direction and a redeeming promise: "All authority in heaven and on earth has been given to me. Go therefore and make disciples of all nations, baptizing them in the name of the Father and of the Son and of the Holy Spirit, and teaching them to obey everything that I have commanded you. And remember, I am with you always, to the end of the age." (Matthew 28:18-20)

Corpus Christi
Mark 14:12-16, 22-26

It's A Small World After All

Lately Jude had spent more and more time with his head resting back against the wall, eyes closed, reliving the Galilee years. He had been counted in that select band of followers who moved with Jesus through the quiet country of the Galilee, and then moved with him into the turbulence of Jerusalem. Jude had always been a friendly type, and his friendship within the disciple band was wide and warm. Indeed, one of the nicknames he held was "the hearty one." He had traveled with Simon on some of his journeys, until Simon was himself crucified. Now in his sixth decade of life, and more easily tired, his time was given to the remembering.

This warm summer day he thought of the last times they had all been together. It was in Jerusalem and in the home of — what was his name? — ah, yes, John Mark's home. It was the meal and the Lord had ended that fellowship time with words that then sounded strange: "Do this in remembrance of me!" Jude could see the room now: the candlelamps that cast moving shadows upon everything, the heat of the evening hour and of the bodies that were lounged around the tiny table in the room's center, the good food, the good company and Jesus' words. As he let his mind search back those 30 years he remembered it as their most special time. And, it had ended so quickly, so brutally. But Jesus had understood what was happening. That is why he said the words, and why the remembering was so important.

Jude, "the hearty one," smiled in the remembering and lifted his arm as if to take the cup from Jesus' outstretched hand. As he did so the iron chains rattled and scraped across the floor. Jude remembered his Lord, and that supper with all those good friends. Because of them chains now held him within a prison cell. But that was all right — really — for Jude had been faithful in that remembering through all the years. And, he knew that he and his Lord were still together, still one body as they had been in the Galilee so long ago. It was all right.

Have you visited Disney World? Our family has, and has taken that scenic ride through the "It's a Small World" exhibit. As the little boat floated along, animated cartoon children from all over the world sang the song and danced in native costumes. At the end of the ride we stepped out of the boat with broad smiles upon our face! It is a delightfully entertaining trip. But the melody, the song "It's a Small, Small World," had been tattooed to the mind — never to be forgotten! For days and weeks afterward I sang to myself,

>   *It's a small world after all.*
>   *It's a small world after all.*
>   *It's a small world after all.*
>   *It's a small, small world!*

There! Now you are tattooed!

We do live in that sort of world: a small, small world. That is not a new idea for any of us. And we really do not need Disney's catchy song to remind us of the fact. Yet, in this small, small world we often do not know much about those who live across town, or outside our block, or beyond our floor in the apartment building. We know where Paris is, but we do not know who a Parisian is. We know the location of China, but we do not know a Chinaman. We know the outline of Russia these days, but we really do not know the spirit of the Russians. We have learned the approximate location of the former Yugoslavia, but do we know what the Serbs are like or the Croats? It is a small world, and getting smaller, but that does not automatically mandate keener knowledge of other people, nor build a deeper interest in other nations, nor sensitize a concern for much beyond our own family and tribe.

Yet there is in the faith surrounding Jesus Christ a universal-mindedness. It does not come naturally, for we frighten too easily. But Jesus Christ calls us to be a single body of humanity created in the spiritual image of God. The Episcopalian chaplain at the University of Chicago (Dr. Sam A. Portaro, Jr.), spoke to a gathering in Cleveland. He said that Jesus' own ministry was judged by his universal-mindedness. "It was the scandal of Jesus' inclusiveness ... that led to his arrest and execution. Jesus would not take sides but struggled always to affirm the wholeness of God's people."

It is that wholeness that can bring us to this moment of the Eucharist. Today's communion table opened on the otherside of the international dateline, on the Tongo Islands, the Figi Islands, New Zealand and Australia. Christians in those distant places took into their hands the elements of bread and wine, and shared with us the remembrance of our Lord. We are brothers and sisters.

And this communion table will not be closed until that dateline is found once again in the Pacific. One 24-hour revolution will see those sharing in our common humanity moving through this common Christian sacrament of remembrance and renewal. All of us all around the world will remember a dark-skinned easterner who took bread and wine, lifted them to symbolize his willing sacrifice, and then commanded that wherever this act would be done that it would be done sharing his real presence. There is nothing like it anywhere — nothing that has such personal unity expressed.

I ask you to hold in your mind and heart this hour that great company of humanity. You and I are but one small part. Yet the Lord Jesus calls us to see that small part as an essential link in the world-wide fellowship of those created in the spirit-image of God.

Think tenderly of those who welcome new life. A baby is a precious thing of immense potential, the focus of love and caring. That wanted child of tender thought may be white or yellow or black or brown or red. Such joy is not measured in color.

Remember during this communion hour people in prison. For some it is a prison of iron bars and electric alarms. Some folks in this congregation work with them in Christ's name. But for many, many others the prison is poverty — which can be just as binding — or a prison of ignorance, or a prison of fear. Hold in your thought and prayer those who fear to leave their homes at night, or who view any person different from themselves as someone of suspicion. Such fears are prison bars.

In this spiritual moment let us remember persons of other religious faiths. So much of the killing these days seems to be in the name of one religion against another. Christ would weep for such angry division in the human family, even as he wept over a city divided and quarrelsome. If only more of the Protestants and Roman Catholics in Ireland could sup together in Jesus' sacrament. If only more Christians and Jews could drink of the cup and eat of the bread. If only more Moslems and Jews could do the same.

In these moments, let us remember children and youth. We have provided them with so much in this nation, lavished out of overflowing abundance. Yet many of them do not think they will have a chance at the good life because of the changes and debts that are now life's story. They have been given so much but, perhaps, robbed of hope. Can we be in handclasp with children and youth in these moments of sacred communion? And they with us?

Let us remember, too, the aged. For some in the fellowship of this communion table life on earth is almost completed. As we drink of the cup and eat of the bread let us remember with love those who have given of themselves, and have now been passed by as the world rushes on. Let not our steps move on without them. They are part of the oneness of this sacrament.

Let us think in this communion time of those persons of earth who may die today because they have no food. We raise money for the hungry but for some it will be too late. A man from the subcontinent of India, on visiting this country for the first time, was asked what surprised him the most about the United States. He said, "The size of your garbage cans."

Think and pray compassionately for the leaders of this world. Whether President or Premier or Secretary General they know burdens beyond our comprehension. In this common moment we would pray God's guidance upon them all — every one.

And let us think of the peoples of the nations, those citizens who support their country because it is their home, their homeland. To speak of home is to speak a universal world. Boundaries are so artificial, mere ink dots upon some paper map. But homeland, that has the pulse of life. Of course, we love our native land. But others do their own, and with the passion we know.

This day the world is at the communion table. Some ignore it, or revile it. But it is a sign of God's love for his world. We are part of it, but only part. We are not in a corner all by ourselves. We are in the middle of life, our life. It is a life shared with more than four billion other persons! It is a small, small world. We must understand that we are not "it," nor are we always right about everything. But here we are, so fortunate, and stewards of the life that God has given us.

We receive the communion with thanksgiving for Jesus Christ our Lord — for his open arms — but we do not receive it alone!

Ordinary Time 9
Mark 2:23—3:6

The M And M Factor

Caleb was probably the laziest boy in the whole village. At least that was his reputation, although no one had ever done scientific study on the question. Caleb could sit in one position — usually, shaded by a tree and upon a matting of soft grass — for hours. He could sit there and watch the clouds move across the sky from daybreak to sunset. Actually, he was never out of bed at day break so the statement was more for effect than truth!

This day Caleb had chosen to escape his field chores by hiding away in his father's grain field. The grain was high enough so that by lying down he was completely hidden. Only the high-flying birds could see him. Which, of course, did not count in any list of possible ways he might be caught. Caleb had really found his place — his youthful resting place.

But suddenly his leisure was destroyed! Sounds of many voices and many feet disturbed his hideaway. And as the voices came closer so did the foot-falls. It sounded as if an army were coming — an army looking for him, he was sure. But before he could run away, the grain around him was parted by an angry crowd who stopped a few feet from him and began shouting. Crouching very still, Caleb shared in an unexpected encounter between Jesus of Nazareth and the religious leaders of his day. Caleb didn't really mean to be part of it. He was caught in the midst of it. Life just moved along, engulfing him, whether he was lazy or not. He long remembered that meeting in the middle of the grain field.

And whether you want to be involved in it today, you are! That is the point. You may have tucked yourself away, but the world comes to you anyway! And you really have to take sides! And, lest you think I am talking of chocolate-coated candy today, I am not.

It is strange to us now, but religion when Jesus encountered the Pharisees was something to be done. Or, better said, something only to be done. Religion then, symbolized by those Pharisees from Jerusalem, was following the good work rules — careful rules, detailed rules, God-oriented rules. On the sabbath one did not work! To make it clearer, so that no one would misunderstand, work was defined by many, many precise definitions, one of which included harvesting — even harvesting grain one kernel at a time by fingertips! In that day you did religion. That is what pleased God, it was then announced.

"Not!" said Jesus, or words to that effect! Religious faith was more than good works! Elsewhere he talked of the two sides of a cup: the inside and the outer side, the motivation and the deed, the thought and the act. The inner beliefs which gave birth to deeds, as well as the deeds themselves. Jesus taught that adultery was not simply an act. Adultery was initially a thought, a plan, a decision of the mind. I believe part of the revival in religious faith in our generation has been this breaking through externals to touch the inner spirit, the soul, the source of belief and motivation. Religion as external observance is not satisfying, nor life-giving when the pressure of living is intense. But when God's Spirit breaks through the externals, then life is entirely different.

Those Pharisees who had traveled from Jerusalem understood that Jesus' way was very different from their way. It was, they believed, the work of Satan, of God's enemy.

As the debate continued, Jesus tried to argue with logic. He thought that it would be a way to reach those learned teachers from the Holy City. Jesus cited the very writings that the Pharisees understood as holy law. King David ate sacred, holy bread when he and his army was hungry. It was bread reserved only for the priests, but King David recognized the human need before the sacramental. That is scripture. (1 Samuel 21) The sabbath is to provide opportunity for humanity to rest and to have time to meditate upon God. "Sabbath was made for humankind, not men and women for the sabbath." (Mark 2:27)

The Pharisees would have nothing to do with such discussion. They continued to hound him. They watched as Jesus' presence in the synagogue brought strength to a man's withered hand. Jesus saw the Pharisees watching and he tried to reason with them once again. "Tell me, Learned Ones," Jesus said, "is it allowed to do good on sabbath?" Jesus knew that the law said it was all right on the sabbath to rescue a cow that had fallen into a ditch. What about a human life? Mark's gospel shares some emotion in the recounting. He says the Pharisees didn't answer Jesus. Jesus "looked around at them with anger, grieved at their hardness of heart." (This is one of the very few references to Jesus' anger.) And so in the presence of the Pharisees from Jerusalem, and in the presence of God's Holy Spirit working through Jesus, the man's arm was strengthened — on the sabbath! Mark then says that the Pharisees plotted how to destroy Jesus.

That is the scripture for today. Now, the M and M factor! It involves siding with the Pharisees or with Jesus.

The Pharisees said one must do religious work to be worthy of God's love and care, to be accepted by God! They spelled out that work with great precision. It had to be precise so that one could know if God really cared for him. This was the reason for the many, many rules and regulations and law that formed the religion of Jesus' day. "You don't work on the sabbath because God won't like you if you do!" Religion involved things that must be done and must not be done.

But, Jesus taught by example that we may do good work as a response to God's love and care that has already been given to us. The healing of that man's arm in the synagogue on the sabbath was done because God's concern for the man willed a strong arm. Jesus knew the power of God's Spirit and he sought to be a channel for that power wherever it could bring God's blessing and goodness upon life. The arm is strengthened. The lame walk. The blind see. The hungry are fed. The despised are befriended. The dying are brought new life. The invitation is extended by Christ: you may choose to do good deeds, as God does good to you. It is the difference between must and may! That is the M and M factor!

This past week some of the committees of our parish have been talking about finances for the year ahead. Budgets are being drawn up. Plans are being laid for the pledge time on November 1st. When we get into these discussions I always think of a man I knew in another church 12 years ago. He had been a salesman all his life and in his later years was disabled by blindness. He was not wealthy although his retirement income was adequate for his care. When I would visit with him he would recount stories of past time when he taught religious instruction, when he helped with this church project or that. One of his sons entered Christian ministry and he was very proud of that. He had been involved with many Christian projects in the community, in addition to his local church work. A community house was of special interest. On one of my visits, he produced a check — one that had a number of zeroes on it — and said that he had some money that he really didn't need and he wanted to share it with some special interests. Would I divide it up and pass it on? Then, pausing in a special reverie all his own, he said, "You know, I have been very, very blessed in my life and I don't have to make these gifts. I just want to give to something that will be of some help to others so that they can someday say how lucky they are." It wasn't anything he had to do! There was no must about it! It was a may, a response to the goodness that he had experienced in life — even in his present blindness!

It is more than money. Giving also involves the resources of thought and experience and prayer and time — all those resources over which we are stewards. You may help with meals on wheels. You may build a house for another person or visit an elderly shut-in person. You may call on a visitor to your church or lead a Bible study time. There is in our response to God's goodness no must. It always is only an invitation.

Christian theologians talk of the Prevenient Grace of God. They mean that God's love comes upon us whether we are deserving of that love or not. God's love comes to us as a grace, a gift that we never earned. We never earn it with a long list of good works, nor a long list of unbroken laws. God's love and care is given to us. Jesus shared that in the strength he gave to the man's withered arm — a strength given even amid the sabbath restrictions thought so important. In response to that grace we may pass on the love to others. God's love does not demand it. That is sometimes a difficult concept to grasp. Edwin Markham understood it when he wrote these four lines:

> *Here is the Truth in a little creed,*
> *　　Enough for all the roads we go:*
> *In Love is all the law we need,*
> *　　In Christ is all the God we know.*

Ordinary Time 10
Mark 3:20-35

Have You Confronted Christ?

Simon bar Jacob — Simon, son of Jacob — had just finished the pruning of his olive trees, ending with the three old trees farthest from the road. He was pleased with his work and looked at it for some time, complimenting himself with satisfying grunts. "Job well done!" He turned to look out upon the full olive grove of 57 trees. Each one had received his careful work, talents learned through the years and taught to him by Jacob, his father. But as he looked toward the roadside near the orchard his heart stopped. There, walking into his orchard was an army of people, a larger crowd than he had ever seen. They filled the spaces between the trees. One young child actually swung from an olive branch, nearly breaking it off, Simon was certain!

The crowd filled the lower part of the orchard and circled round so that they all were in sound-reach of the man who now sat upon a ridge of rocks that Simon had gleaned from the soil. Simon began to run toward the crowd, uncertain of what he would do or say but certain of his desire to protect his property, his inheritance of olive trees. He broke into a run and was quickly at the outskirts of the crowd. But his initial fears and anger were quieted when he saw that he knew many of the folks now gathered around the teacher. "They will not hurt my orchard," he thought. "I know them."

And he was right. Although they stayed for most of the day, not one branch was broken. Nor did the young boys climb the trees. Soon Simon was listening to the teacher and sharing in that special moment when Jesus, from nearby Nazareth, taught about God. It was said by those standing with Simon that Jesus' own family was part of the crowd. It was said they had followed him from Nazareth, hoping that he would come back with them and back to the work and into the protection of Nazareth. Jesus was gaining too much attention by the things he did and the words he spoke. He was not as he once had been. His family was worried. But in the press of people Simon never discovered who they were.

What he did discover was that shortly after noon, a silence fell upon the crowd. It was a silence that began along the road's edge and worked its way through the crowd until it reached Jesus. Priests from the temple in Jerusalem had entered the orchard. Their presence brought a hush upon the crowd. Unlike Jesus' family they were easily seen! Their dress was elaborate. Their head wrapping was of finest cloth. Their step was like that of royalty, expecting adulation. The look upon their faces was of great disdain, but edged with fear for they were in a foreign setting. They could not have remembered when they last walked in an olive orchard. Those priests came close to Jesus and the leader pointed a jeweled finger to the teacher's face. "You are possessed by Beelzebub," he said. As if to second the motion, another priest quickly shouted, "The ruler of demons casts out demons!"

Simon bar Jacob — Simon, son of Jacob — remembered the silence of that confrontation that took place amid the ripening trees of his orchard. He was there and he found that he, too, had to decide about Jesus.

Twenty centuries later, you and I share that moment of confrontation. That is the point of this sermon from these verses in Mark's gospel! That is the point of the Christian faith! Each of us is involved in the confrontation.

The confrontation came early and with great force in Jesus' ministry. As Mark tells the story, Jesus had just chosen his disciples. He had just begun his teaching times, and word spread quickly that his touch could heal broken lives. The crowds were eager to hear him and to receive from him. The beginning verse of the text tells of it, "the crowd came together again so that they could not even eat."

That word sped quickly to Jerusalem. Included within that word was the accusation that Jesus' newly-appointed disciples picked grain on the sabbath — they broke the law! — and that Jesus had healed a "withered hand" on the sabbath. — Again, the law had been broken! Something must be done! The religion of law — only law — was threatened! And so the Pharisees traveled down from their high, holy city. They accused Jesus of being possessed by Satan. Jesus was God's enemy. The gauntlet had been thrown down upon the dusty road in the Galilee! Sides had to be chosen, decisions made.

Jesus countered, if Satan is evil, how can Satan do good? This is schizophrenic! Jesus did not use that word! He did say a kingdom divided against itself cannot stand, which is a fair definition of that word. This was not discussion over some small point of religious law. This was debate over change — great change. Little wonder that Jesus' family wanted to hurry him away to the protection of his home.

Midway into this confrontation Jesus said a very harsh thing. What did he mean when he said, "Whoever blasphemes against the Holy Spirit can never have forgiveness, but is guilty of an eternal sin?" (Mark 3:28-29) One commentator, Halford E. Luccock, noted that this is one of the things he wishes Jesus had never said.

Jesus' statement has produced hard emotional scars upon some sensitive persons. Not many months ago I had a conversation with a man who was deeply disturbed. He was emotionally sick. He needed professional counseling — much more than I could provide. What he continually talked about was his belief that he had committed that eternal sin, that unpardonable sin. He never shared what it was or what he believed it was. "I just can't speak it," he said. It was a thought that he had held since his youth, and for thinking that terrible thought he believed Jesus was condemning him eternally. The whole gospel message was — for him — focused on that single verse, that single eternal condemnation by Jesus. I worry about how such a phrase is taught to young people, to young lives just forming serious religious understandings. Biblical literalists, from their position of self-confidence, refer to it as if that single verse stands all by itself.

But Jesus' word is part of the total confrontation that took place that day. The religiously learned stood before Jesus and condemned him for doing good, because it was done on the Sabbath; condemned his followers for the simple act of plucking heads of grain on the sabbath; condemned the common people of that day for their lack of righteousness because they did not follow the religious law with the exactness that they (the religiously learned) followed it. Indeed, the word pharisee comes from separated ones. Those richly-robed leaders were proud of their separation from the sinful common people, from those contaminated by the world. In their haughty separateness, the Pharisees had become so blind that they called the good works of God to be the works of Satan! "The essence of their sin is callous blindness." *(Cambridge Bible Commentary on Mark*, page 32) "The sin for which there was no forgiveness was just what the scribes were doing when Jesus spoke the words — calling good evil." *(Interpreter's Bible,* Vol. 7, page 693) That religious elite was so caught in pride and self-interest that it labeled what was divine as satanic! That was the sin. The religious ones were so tied up in their sense of religious rules that even great good to human life, taught by Jesus as God's good gift, could be seen only as the act of evil. That, said Jesus, in that moment of confrontation, was unpardonable!

But I find another message in this confrontation. In the sharpness of the words exchanged on that ancient day we may overlook a wonderful spiritual forest because of this single textual tree! Through his deeds and in his word here, Jesus is also affirming the wideness of God's mercy and love and forgiveness! God's forgiveness is part of that great expansive good open to every human life. So much of our human sin and error is redeemable! If only this narrow, myopic sin of the scribes and Pharisees is unpardonable, then so much more is pardonable!

That message is one to be shared far and wide. That is good news. Jesus is saying that there is a release from guilt that is offered. Jesus is saying that there is the possibility of a "new start" with our Heavenly Father. Is that the message of the faith you need to hear today?

Some orders of worship include what is titled Words of Assurance. They are scripture words telling the chance of forgiveness:

> *"The Lord is gracious and merciful, slow to anger and abounding in steadfast love."*
> — Psalm 148:08

> *"If we confess our sins, he is faithful and just, and will forgive our sins and cleanse us from all unrighteousness."*
> — 1 John 1:09

Our confrontation with Jesus Christ opens to each of us the blessed opportunity of forgiveness, and in that unburdening, the opportunity for a new start in our relationship to God and to one another.

I hope and pray that the broken and sick man, burdened beyond his ability to cope by that single verse, was eventually able to see the broader landscape of God's great love and forgiveness — that landscape lived and shared through Jesus Christ. For in that larger land is his hope — and ours!

Ordinary Time 11
Mark 4:26-34

Pathway To God's Kingdom

Jacob knew nothing of the geography that stretched beyond his farmland to the Great Sea. He did not even know that a Great Sea existed out there, westward beyond his land. He had never been further than half a day's journey from the collection of 15 stone houses that formed his village. Nor did he know anyone who had been further away than those eight or 10 miles. Nor did anyone in his village think much about far-off regions. Jacob only knew of the fields and gentle slopes of land that he could see as he paused in the hard work of seed planting. While he did not know of the far reaching geography, Jacob did know about seedtime and harvest. And he knew his limits!

Once the winter rains had slowed, Jacob would prepare the ground for the planting. But before he started the work he fasted, preparing himself for the task of preparing the land. It was a prescribed rite (Deuteronomy 16:13), ancient and mystical. The farm tool that he used was almost as ancient. It was a thick, heavy tree limb, tipped with iron, given to him by his father years earlier. The donkey pulled it, with Jacob ever forcing it into the earth. Together they would break the clods of earth, turning the grasses inward. His field work took more than the days between two Sabbaths to finish — that with good weather, too. When the ground was broken he would place the carefully stored seed into a bag that he slung over one shoulder. Then, as he walked back and forth across his field, he would "broadcast" that precious seed. Each handful would be thrown with a sweeping swing of his arm. When he reached the far side of his field, the planting was done.

With the tasks completed, Jacob looked to the heavens, but not with the eye of a modern agronomist and meteorologist who could calculate studied prescriptions of soil quality and weather to come. His look was of resignation. He had done his part, the only part he could do. Now God would do the growing. In his understanding, the land he worked was a gift from God! (Deuteronomy 11:8) It did not really belong to him, nor did all the crops that came from his work.

But one day the ordinary routine of farming in Jacob's village was broken. It was broken when the Rabbi came along the path from the Great Sea, from Nazareth although Jacob had not known a Nazareth existed. The Rabbi stopped at Jacob's field to talk and to teach. Jacob remembered that moment for the rest of his life.

Others remembered it, too. Years later they remembered Jesus' seed-teaching in terms of the growing of God's kingdom upon earth. The divine in life grows. The heavenly on earth develops, like a seed growing toward maturity. God's kingdom on earth was a very important part of Jesus' teaching and so, "Come, let us walk in the way of the Lord."

God's kingdom, by that title, is not mentioned in the Old Testament, and is seldom mentioned in the New Testament except in the synoptics. In the gospel of John it is cited only twice. In the book of Acts, describing the beginnings of the Christian church, it is only noted six times. But the kingdom of God is a central part of the synoptic tradition, that collection of preaching found in Matthew, Mark and Luke. Jesus' preaching, as remembered in Matthew, Mark and Luke, is filled with illustrations of God's rule upon earth, God's kingdom.

His teaching is understood as both something about to happen (imminent) and as something already arrived! God's kingdom is imminent as in the Lord's Prayer, "Thy kingdom come, thy will be done on earth as it is in heaven." (Luke 11:02) Jesus also taught us to understand that God's kingdom is already a present reality. He spoke to the Pharisees, "In fact, the kingdom of God is among you." (Luke 17:21) In a paradoxical way, that seems true to life. God's working presence seems always to do with the immediate moment as well as pulling us into a greater fulfillment in the faith. The now is blessed by God. The call of God moves us into greater blessings — ultimately, from the kingdom upon earth to the kingdom of heaven.

Through two parables Jesus taught of this kingdom.

The kingdom of God is mysterious growth. We do not have all the answers, there is always mystery with life, yet that does not keep the kingdom from being a reality. It is like a farmer, Jesus said, who plants the seed and then goes to sleep, goes away someplace, and the life within the seed brings forth the shoots, then the plants, then the harvest. (Mark 4:26-29) How? Even the farmer does not know. It is mysterious growth.

You and I who are parents have seen this mysterious growth as a tiny baby grows through childhood, through youth, and then into the possibilities of adulthood. As I see my children grow, I marvel. Can they be the little babies, so helpless, that once upon a time began life. I suspect that every parent looks at a child in such a wonder.

What we can see in physical growth, and marvel at, is also the story of spiritual growth, and of the growth of God's kingdom! The disciple band that clustered about Jesus revealed that growth. At first they were workmen, toiling at daily tasks. Then they became students, disciples of their Lord. As they grew in understanding about God's kingdom they also misunderstood. They denied knowledge of their confessed Master. In fear, they hid because of him. But as their growth continued they moved out of their hiding to be called, not disciples, but apostles, speakers for their Lord.

This spiritual growth is part of this parish these days. Through some of the religious instruction classes, through the

Bible studies, through our youth group, through the many caring ministries of the people of this church, a spiritual renaissance is marked upon many persons here! It is the kingdom of God, growing in ways we cannot fully comprehend now. All we know is that the seeds, once planted, are growing.

The kingdom of God, in this mysterious growth, becomes something of great worth and service. It is like the tiny mustard seed, when planted, growing into a great bush that is part of the value of nature. Even the birds of the air can use its protection for nesting. (Mark 4:30-32)

I want to tell you an incredible story about the mysterious growth of God's kingdom that resulted in a gift of great worth. It is not, like that of Jacob the farmer, a make-believe story. This is a true story about another Jacob!

On April 18, 1942, into gun-gray sky, sixteen B-25 planes took off from a pitching aircraft-carrier deck and headed for Japan. They were under the command of Jimmy Doolittle. Those 16 planes planned a surprise attack upon the Japanese mainland, as the Japanese had done to Pearl Harbor only five months earlier. Beginning about noon that April 18th they made their strike and then, because of low fuel, continued on to the China mainland. The fuel ran out and in bad weather the planes crashed. Most of those airmen were saved by friendly forces, but two of the planes crashed on Japanese-held land. Both crews were captured. The crew of one plane was killed. The crew of the other plane — plane No. 16 named "Bat Out Of Hell" — was held prisoner throughout the war. One of the five-man crew died in captivity. The others were released a few days after the atomic destruction of Nagasaki on August 9, 1945.

One of the survivors was Jacob DeShazer. He was bombadier of that plane No. 16. DeShazer's three years of captivity was the story of depravation, torture and untreated illness. More than 70 boils covered his body. He became weak from dysentery. From the depth of that hell, he searched for God. He later said, "The way the Japanese treated me I had to turn to Christ. No matter what they did to me, I prayed. I prayed for strength to live. And I prayed for the strength, somehow, to find forgiveness for what they were doing to me."

Somewhere in his youth small seeds of God's work through Jesus Christ had been planted. I do not know that even he could identify the planter or the planting time. It may have been a parent in discussion about God's kingdom present within a human life. It may have been a church school teacher teaching a lesson from the very parables that we study now. It may have been a neighbor, a preacher, a peer in his youth. Somehow, in that mystery of spiritual influence, the seed was planted that allowed Jacob DeShazer to struggle with the mysterious growth of God's kingdom in his own life, a growth that took place in a prison cell! (How God's kingdom grows in times of difficulty, oppression, imprisonment — whether physical or emotional.)

After his release DeShazer became a Christian missionary. For three decades he strove to bring the beliefs of God's kingdom to China and Japan. But that seed continued to grow. In a curious twist, Jacob DeShazer was instrumental in the conversion of Mitsuo Fuchida, the Japanese flier who had led the air attack on Pearl Harbor. In time, Mitsuo Fuchida, himself, became a Christian minister to his people in Japan.

Jesus taught about a tiny seed, once planted, growing in mysterious, unaccountable, ways to become something of great worth to the world. In such a way, he said, God's kingdom is all around us and within us!

Of course, we cannot study Jesus' teaching of God's rule without learning the big message that you and I are centrally involved in it! Jesus believed so strongly that God's kingdom was the means of fulfilling God's creation. That blessed kingdom offers the completion of God's creation, moving from earth to heaven. The kingdom offers all that God desires for us. As we seek to walk close to Jesus we are part of God's work through Jesus — we are within the kingdom. And so the invitation is always given, "Come, let us walk in the way of the Lord!" That invitation is to be very attentive to the days of this week. Every day you are sharing in the planting of seeds of God's love and kingdom. But more, you will receive, this week, the blessing of other plantings. Those blessings are part of the walk, too. Through it all, you are growing toward the harvest time — in your living now, and in your claim to that eternal kingdom of God's great love. It is mystery. It is growth.

Ordinary Time 12
Mark 4:35-41

Walking Through A Storm

Simon was in control of the boat. He was the oldest, and besides it was his boat. He had sailed the waters so often, and usually at night because that is when most of the fishing took place. The disciples pushed away from the shore, a shore still crowded with the village people. The sun had set but still cast a warm, red glow over the hillside, over the men, women and children who had come to hear Jesus and to be healed. The sun's glow worked out upon the gently moving sea. It may have been John, the youngster, who was last into the boat. His push was the final one freeing it from the gravel along the shore. Soon a small sail was raised. Soon the noise of the crowd was gone. Soon the rocking sea quieted the men and allowed their Master to dip his head in sleep. Soon the glow of the sun was gone. Soon the stars filled the dark sky. Soon, too, the clouds came with the wind. Soon the gentle waves became a churning and dangerous sea. Simon's voice was not as steady, which quickened a sense of fear among the others. Soon Simon's voice was not even heard, nor hearable.

The dark sky seemed to dip down and touch the waves. The wind from distant Mount Hermon rushed upon the disciples as they frantically lowered the sail and bailed water from the boat's bottom. Light was present only because of the lightning. It cast momentary shadows and lighted the white edges of the waves that rushed against the side of the boat. Those lightning flashes also revealed frightened faces. Even the elder Simon's face showed the terror of the rough sea. Yet, the Master slept, still rocked by the motion of the waters. In the midst of that great danger, the Master was calm in his rest.

The Sea of Galilee is known for its sudden storms. The disciples were in the midst of one and it was greater than they had experienced. They didn't know what to do. Those fishermen of the quiet waters were now in a turbulent storm, fearful for their lives. Those experienced workmen of a calm Galilee now faced something very different. And that makes it our story, too!

At one time or another, all of us are afloat on a troubled sea. Worry. Uncertainty. Tangled troubles. Fear. We want the Master to wake up! We want him to quiet the churning waters that are all around us. We want him to solve our problems! We're seasick with worry, with pain, with tension, with fear. "Wake up, Jesus. We're in trouble. Save us!"

When was that last your cry? Life is not always like a calm sea. We are not always rested by the gentle wake. There is much that disturbs us! Each evening, the television news of our city reports sudden death. In the United States there were 23,000 murders last year. Life comes to a sudden end, with finality and brutality. That feeds our fear!

We are frightened by an unknown future in an ever-changing world. Dr. Elizabeth Tracy, a professor at Case Western Reserve University, reported on the changing family. Only 10 percent of families today are of the traditional variety, with father working, mother at home, and marriage of lifelong commitment. In this changing nation, there are 1,300 "step families" formed each day. Dr. Tracy, a teacher of social work, reported that children in step families need at least six years to adapt to the changes that have occurred in their lives! She said, "Average married persons today — because of multiple marriages — have more parents than children!" That is something new for us to handle, and its newness feeds the worry, the fear.

We are afloat on a troubled sea, and we cry out for Jesus to wake up and save us!

We physically hurt! The pain, deep inside that comes upon us in the dark of the night, is fraught with worry. Our bodies are not immune to disease nor aging. Each day might bring a diagnosis we do not want to hear. Nor do we want to hear that health care costs rose twenty-two percent last year! That is a deep problem for some folks. Other people know another health worry, for they are part of the 40 million Americans who have no health insurance! The storms swirl around us.

And, we emotionally hurt! In our fast-paced world we can so easily be cut apart by the words that others speak or the prejudices that slice into great groups of people. We are not all Hollywood starlets, nor built like some Greek god. We are not all brilliant in mind nor quick in speech. We do not all make friends so rapidly, nor bond so easily. The emotional side of life can be for us the same as that storm up on the Galilee Sea. And we cry for Jesus to wake up and make things right!

Mark's gospel tells us that Jesus did just that! He spoke to the storm and it quieted. He said, "Peace. Be still." And, writes Mark, "there was a great calm." In our modern, scientific way of thinking, we do not easily understand all this. Storms upon seas are caused by wind currents, temperature differences and open spaces. A recent news article told of this climatic possibility on the Sea of Galilee, triggered by the winds coming off of Mount Hermon and moving down upon the waters. Storms just are not controlled by someone's shout off the back end of a boat. But that is the recounting that Mark gives — and Matthew (8:18) and Luke. (8:22)

Some students of the Bible and of psychology have suggested that Jesus' word to the wind and rain, giving his witness to God's care, calmed his disciples so that they could then tackle the storm! That may have been Jesus' greater power. He infused those trembling disciples with a calmness to see the storm through. I have seen that happen! I suspect you have, too!

I have seen that spirit-word of Jesus take hold of a sobbing and broken woman whose husband had just then been pronounced dead. "Peace. Be still." In ways that I cannot explain, she was empowered to move through the difficult days that his death brought. His death came so suddenly, leaving her with young children and much debt. Later, with grown children around her, she said, "I remembered Jesus' words and I figured he was talking to me."

Another person, upon learning that his employment ceased with the next paycheck, thought of the faith witness, "The Lord is my shepherd, I shall not want." (Psalm 23) It became his theme song through difficult days, but days that he did not walk alone. "That shepherd was, for me, Jesus," he said. "And it was Jesus who taught us not to worry about our life." Indeed, that was Jesus' word upon the hillside, "Therefore I tell you, do not worry about your life, what you will eat or what you will drink, or about your body, what you will wear. Is not life more than food, and the body more than clothing?" (Matthew 6:25) It is a conscious shift of mental emphasis.

The ultimate teaching of Jesus — which Jesus was living out in that storm-tossed boat — was of God's good care! The birds of the air are in God's care. The little children are in God's good care. The ill, the aged, the lonely — all are in God's good care. And when the storm is heavy, even when a cross is lifted to the dark sky, it is Jesus' faith that God's good care is there. It is a conscious shift of emphasis from self to God.

I have known that in my own life. There have been times when things were dark, when it appeared I was ensnared, and when there was no tunnel to the light. Then, in the darkness, came a sense that God would see me through. I did not know how. I could not imagine how! But faith in that care has not let me down. For some here, that is your story, too. One of our hymns gives that faith. It was written by Civilla Martin on a Sunday afternoon. She was ill, bed-bound. Her husband composed the tune later that day. It is, says one book, "a hymn of comfort."

Be not dismayed what e'er betide,
God will take care of you;
Beneath his wings of love abide,
God will take care of you.

"Peace," said Jesus. "Be still!"

But we must understand the role of the messenger as well as the message. For the disciples, the power of the peace came through Jesus' words. For the woman whose husband died, peace came through the persons who shared her grief. For that gentleman out of work it came through one close friend. For me it came through a circle of family and a few friends who shared their faith. At one time or another, each of us must be the Master's voice to someone else in a storm! It is so very comforting to hear the Master talk to the particular sea that is upsetting us. It is nice, and so calming, to hear Christ's word upon our predicament. "Be still!" The disciples were calmed by Jesus. But we also are called to share the word of faith.

Remember a later New Testament story. It was of another disciple, Paul, who spoke words of calm to a frightened man. It was not upon Lake Galilee. It was in a dark prison cell during the hell that followed a night-time earthquake in Philippi! (Acts 16:16-40) Silas and Paul were on a missionary journey, traveling over to the European mainland. They had converted the wealthy woman, Lydia. They had met a slave girl who was earning her master a great fortune by telling fortunes. The slave girl was changed by the work of Paul and Silas, which meant a recession in the economy of her owners. They had the disciples thrown into a Philippian prison. In the dark of night an earthquake broke open the prison gates and the jailer assumed all the prisoners had fled to freedom. In the turbulance of that thought he was about to take his own life. But a voice was heard from the depths of the prison, "Do not harm yourself, for we are all here." It was a word to the jailer as powerful as the words Jesus uttered to the sea. Through the voice of Paul, it was the Master's voice initiating a new life for that jailer.

Part of this spirit-ministry in the midst of the storm is that other persons reach out to touch the hurting life, the worried life, the broken life. It is called caring for one another. And it is a blessing shared through the human family. For Christians it is the expression of Christ in our humanity. For some of us this caring is in boxes of food that this day sail upon another sea on a journey to Moscow. Our caring is rooted in our Lord's faith in his Heavenly Father's caring.

Indeed, the storms of life have, for many persons, been the way by which God has opened new and blessed relationships. The dark cloud does have a silver lining! Someone should write a song about that! On one occasion, my wife and I were flying into Washington, D.C. It was one of those flights that are so common today. To get from point A to point B one must, of necessity, go through point C. Washington D.C. was point C between Cleveland and Orlando. The closer we got to Washington and the lower we flew, the evidence of humanity was all about. Ribbons of roads tied together towns and cities. Great shopping malls nested in acres of asphalt. Row after row of houses were clustered near interstate entrance ramps. And, off in the distance I saw a brilliant light shining. It was like a huge diamond set amid a small pine forest. The sunlight danced as it was reflected back to my window in the plane. As the plane circled around for the approach, those diamond lights continued to send strong beams skyward. What could be producing such brilliance and beauty amid the forest land? As the plane got lower on the approach I saw that it was a junk yard. Those diamonds set amid the pines were the mangled metal and broken glass of humanity's highway wrecks. But still, in the tangle of trouble represented in that junk yard, beauty could be discovered.

The thought crossed my sermonic mind that amid the human pain and worry and fear, with the voice of Christ speaking his faith in God's care, there is to be discovered something of value, even of beauty. Christ said, "Peace. Be still." There was great calm. The fierce sea did not destroy. Life was not lost! The faith held.

Ordinary Time 13
Mark 5:21-43

Living By
Faith And Trust

Jairus' little daughter was the sweetest child in the whole village. Everyone said so. She was slight in build and shy in behavior. And she was kind, more kind than any of the other children. Everyone said that, too. So when she fell ill and could not even venture beyond the framing of the front door of her house everyone in the town was greatly concerned. Her parents were well-respected, for her father was one of the 10 men in town who ruled the synagogue. He had lived within the bounds of the town all his life. If anyone had a problem — any sort of problem — they sought out Jairus. He was kindly, like his daughter, and fair and he knew the holy writings. Many times he had given the advice to pray to Almighty God. "The Lord God will attend to your prayer," he would say. And he believed it.

Now, with his tiny daughter lying motionless upon the pallet in the corner of his house, Jairus was confounded that his prayers did not seem to matter. He, along with the whole town, was in great turmoil of spirit. So, when the word reached him that Jesus was nearby he ran to him, pleading for any help that Jesus might offer. "My little daughter is at the point of death." What father would not be anguished to utter such a sentence?

But amid the anguish that he and his town shared, there was the spirit-flame of hope that still gave some light. "If you touch her, she will be made well!" In that faith Jairus moved with Jesus toward the house, walking through the crowds of women who had already begun the death wails. At the end of their journey, the little 12-year-old daughter walked with them. The faith of Jairus held true.

Let us talk of faith. There was another little girl. She was about eight years of age. She had lived all those years within the loving embrace of the Christian church. Her whole family was involved: mother, father, sister and herself. Within that church family she became acquainted with a lady who lived on her street. They were good friends. The lady was always at the church when the little girl was there. Every Sunday morning they met at church. But the lady's husband was not at church. He was never there. The little girl knew the husband, for she had visited in their home. But she never saw that husband in the church with his wife. One day, in quiet innocence, that little girl asked her lady friend, "Where does your husband go to church?" All the people that little girl knew went to church someplace. The reply was unexpected! "Sweetie," the lady friend replied, "he doesn't go to church anyplace." Then there was a great silence. Finally the little girl, having grasped this new and unexplained information, asked, "Does he cuss?"

That is a true story. I know the little girl. And it is not really a word about the husband who does not attend church. It is an interchange about those of us who do go to church. Expressed in thought and words of an eight-year-old child is a statement about those who do frequent churches. It is a story about the image of a Christian . . . the definition of a Christian faith put into everyday action. I invite us all to follow up on that this morning. What is it that makes Christians different? How might we frame a definition?

There are some folks who think that a simple affirmation is all that is necessary. "Do you believe in Jesus?" "Yes, I do!" "Fine, you're a Christian!" With the words, "I believe," or "Jesus is Lord," or "Jesus saves me," then all that is needed has somehow been done. The achievement has been made. Heaven is assured. The lifestyle, the attitudes, the behavior beyond that affirmation do not matter essentially, for the "acceptance of Christ" has assured all that really matters — so some people say.

Back in the Middle Ages it played out as a game. The words of faith were spoken from the deathbed, but not a moment sooner. It made for the best of both worlds, so thought the angler of those Middle Ages. Unfortunately, there remains some of that simplistic sentiment today. Religious "code words" do not a Christian make.

Whereas there are some people who think that only a repetition of words is necessary, so there are other folks who think that Jesus' ethical example is the sole key. All that is needed to make the Christian is to be a "little Jesus" in word and action. Do as Jesus did!

This, too, falls far short. If we earnestly seek to duplicate Jesus' earthly behavior we will inevitably meet with failure. The most earnest of saints in past ages have tried this, only to be engulfed in frustration and despair at failure. The Methodist story of John Wesley's search to do better in good deeds, even sailing the Atlantic to convert the American Indians, is the story of this futility. A working Christian faith does not come to birth in trying to mimic Jesus' life.

There must be something beyond the "Good Word Speakers" and the "Good Deed Doers."

The one point of this homily is that the keystone of Christian faith is a trust in God and in that life that God has given us through Christ Jesus! That is the mark, the clue. That is the ground from which the Christian life grows productive and contented and moral. That is the ground from which faith grows more deeply. This trust in God provides the beginnings for an assurance that the essentials of life do not end with earth's death. This trust in God opens eternity.

Jesus showed this! He lived with such faith and trust in God that nothing could defeat him. It was a faith and trust that prompted his good deeds, out of a shear gratitude to God for the gift of life. It was a faith and trust that carried him through trials and rejections. It was a faith and trust that opened to him the windows of eternity. In a moment of fear upon the heavy seas of Galilee, Jesus slept in the back of the boat. Later he quieted the fears of those distraught and sweating disciples. (Mark 4:35-41)

Jesus taught this! Standing on the edge of some Galilean field he said, "Consider the lilies of the field; they do not work, they do not spin, yet I tell you even Solomon in all his splendor was not attired like one of these ... But if that is how God clothes the grass of the fields ... will God not all the more clothe you? How little faith (trust) you have." (Matthew 5:28) How do you answer?

Is not this trust in God the root of Jesus' statement that each one of us must take on certain child-like qualities if we would inherit the good that God has provided for us? I read his teaching, "You must have the trust of a little child before God's kingdom can come to you."

The text today is about a man who faced a great, great difficulty. It was a potential tragedy that few persons have to face — the death of his child. While Mark's gospel does not give us a clinical report on the illness or the recovery, what is very clear is that Jairus' faith in Jesus and the Lord God that Jesus proclaimed told him that his daughter would be made well. It was not a half-hearted faith. Scripture says that Jairus asked Jesus, "Come and lay your hands on her, so that she may be made well and live." (5:23) It was a strong expectation of Jesus' power. It was the same faith held by that nameless woman who interrupted their journey to the little girl. She was a woman who believed that with just one touch of Jesus' garment she would be healed. And, it happened! Jesus responded, "Woman, your faith, your trust has cured you." (5:34)

It was this sort of faith and trust in God's care that empowered Jesus' first disciples. Paul would soon write: "We are troubled on every side, yet not distressed. We are perplexed, but not in despair; persecuted, but not forsaken; cast down, but not destroyed." (2 Corinthians 4:08) Is that your faith . . . your trust?

The early writing of the church gave some formal definitions: "Faith gives substances to our hopes. Makes us certain of realities that we do not see." (Hebrews 11:01) And, in the next chapter of Hebrews, the writing directs that we must "throw off every encumbrance, weight; and run with resolution the race set for us." (Hebrews 12:01) Encumbrances diminish faith. Fear diminishes faith. Hate, too, is a weight upon us, as is worry and distrust. And so the message comes at us from many directions: Have faith in God's care. Trust God and the life God has given in Christ Jesus.

Yet, there are some folks, some we know, who have little or no trust, whose lives are filled with complaint and bitterness. Even the American Medical Association says that will kill you!

An old southern evangelist was preaching up a storm and ended his long sermon by asking the people to come to the front of the church and give testimony to what God had done for them. People responded, speaking their strong and positive testimony, but not enough of them to the liking of the evangelist. So, he began to call upon them by name. "Brother Smith, what has God done for you?" Finally he got down to Uncle Harry, an old man, sitting to the side, crippled up with all sorts of ailments, blind in one eye, hard of hearing. "Uncle Harry," he shouted, "what has the Lord done for you?" Uncle Harry laboriously raised himself with the help of his cane and the pew in front, looked up at the evangelist, and shouted back, "Well, he's just about done me in!" There are some folks, far less troubled than Uncle Harry, who claim to be Christian yet concentrate on that same done-in condition. But that is not the message of faith from the Bible, even when spoken by Uncle Harry from the pew of a church.

We seek to hold faith, trust in God and the life through Christ that God has given.

Not far from this place is a woman friend of mine who is crippled beyond imagination. She is alone most of the day and very helpless. Only with a large-button telephone by her side can she call for help. She lives in a country setting. But her witness is that she is not alone. She has a faith and trust in God who cares for her in spirit. Those who volunteer to help her from time to time admit that she helps them far more ... because of her faith and trust in God.

In the late evening in a hospital I prayed with a man about to undergo cancer surgery. He did not have any idea how it would turn out that next morning. As we held hands during those moments of prayer, he said, "I don't worry. I have always known that life is a gift to me. I have always believed in God's care. I have no reason to change my mind now, no matter what happens tomorrow."

I read of a man who died and left his possessions to his children. The heritage was carefully listed in the will. But a final paragraph made that will different from most others. This is what he had written: "I desire also to bequeath to my children and their families my testimony to the truth and preciousness of the gospel of Jesus Christ. This heritage of the Christian faith, received in unbroken line from the apostles and prophets and martyrs, is of infinitely more value than any house or automobile or land or material possession. I hereby bequeath it to them all." Trust in God and the life that God has given through Christ. Is that you?

Beloved brothers and sisters in Christ: the message is, seek to live by faith and trust in God. That is the mark. In that, the Christian life is found ... and it is very good!

Ordinary Time 14
Mark 6:1-6

Walking
The Familiar

There was still a slick of morning moisture covering the path into the town as Eli and Samuel walked by Nathan's orchard, crossed the small stream, and finished the prescribed sabbath day's journey to the synagogue: in length, 2,000 cubits. By our modern standard of travel it was not far. It was about 1,000 yards. They walked at hurried pace. Their prayer shawls were pulled tightly around them, which helped protect them from the morning chill. Sabbath. The day of rest. In Nazareth the gathering was a comfortable event. Everyone knew everyone, and most knew what the others would do or say, such as the fact that Eli and Samuel were always the last to take their seats. The complaints, the prayers, the remembered verses of the holy writings, it all unfolded each seventh day as if written in some careful text. Eli and Samuel lived the farthest from the synagogue and so it was expected that they would be the last to arrive. They always were. The path they took was so familiar that even Samuel could have walked it alone. And Samuel was blind.

This day as the familiar men of Nazareth sat in their accustomed places, and as the anticipated words were said, and as the routine of sabbath moved along its appointed course, it all was broken by the words of a young workman. The young carpenter, now turned traveling preacher, spoke up in the midst of the sabbath synagogue routine. He spoke up, as he never had done before, with quotations from ancient prophets seldom heard within that place. He left the very vivid impression that he was not just talking ancient words. He spoke with eloquence and with directness. Even blind Samuel cocked his head in a way that showed his attention! And there was a frown upon his brow! With the words spoken by the carpenter, the comfortable routines of sabbath and the ordinary expectations of the town folk had been broken! Samuel leaned toward Eli and with a voice heard by more than Eli, said, "Who is this person to speak so? What right does he have to voice such words here in our synagogue?" Eli whispered back some of the things he had heard about Jesus. Others joined in the recounting. But their reports were couched in modern tabloid words, not in holy words nor in words spoken like the honored scribes.

They just did not like the ease of their sabbath broken. They liked the routines which brought comfort in ways they could not articulate. Something was different here. Something new! And frankly, they did not like it. This new preacher in their midst was just the carpenter, the son of Mary. His brothers and sisters were known throughout Nazareth. Nice people — all of them. But he should not speak so forthrightly! It was not seemly on this nice sabbath day to break from the comfortable traditions. And so that congregation in Nazareth took offense at Jesus.

———————

The little imagined story of Eli and Samuel is to bring us to the scripture, a story to describe some of the humanness of that day when Jesus entered the hometown synagogue and scored a zero. Mark's gospel, as well as Matthew's, does not tell what Jesus said when he spoke in his hometown synagogue. Luke's gospel does. Luke tells that he read these words from the sacred scroll of the prophet Isaiah:

> *The Spirit of the Lord is upon me, because he has anointed me to bring good news to the poor. He has sent*

> *me to proclaim release to the captives and recovery of sight to the blind, to let the oppressed go free, to proclaim the year of the Lord's favor!*
> — Isaiah 61:1

Mark does tell that this visit comes midway in Jesus' ministry. Jesus was heralded as a great teacher and healer throughout the region, except in his hometown. In Mark, the verses immediately preceding today's scripture tell of the wonderment in restoring life to Jairus' young daughter. And there were other healings, and great words of teaching. Now Jesus is back home in Nazareth. It is the sabbath. Jesus is in the synagogue participating as a man of the faith. But "they took offense at him." Those are Mark's words!

The people attending synagogue that day were so caught up in looking backward that they could not look into the future. Jesus was still only the child of former days, and the people were so stilted in the rote of the service, that they just could not understand anything new. And so "they took offense at him."

Jesus "marveled at their unbelief." Those, too, are Mark's words. This rejection in his hometown pushed aside any possibility of new understanding of Jesus, and of the good news he spoke.

With this rejection in Nazareth, Jesus now turns to a new pattern of mission. He sends out the disciples two by two. They are to go where they will be accepted! They are to speak the good news and do the good deeds that Jesus himself set out to do. The words they all were to speak were words about repentance, which means, "turn about, change the direction of your life!" The deeds were the charity of healing, of making whole, lives that were broken or limited. These verses mark Jesus' first rejection, and his first organized mission endeavor fueled by that rejection. It all happened because, in his hometown, the folks were short-sighted, and were so tied to the familiar, the ordinary.

Thus far, we have talked of ancient happenings. Let us bring Eli and Samuel, and others of that congregation, into our day! For me these verses speak both a warning and a wonderment.

The warning is that we can let routines hide God from our sight. The comfort of routines can hinder the work of God.

I recently heard a beautiful new hymn from Korean translation. Americans are not familiar with the tune, nor with the words. It breaks the comfortable tradition of familiar hymns. How might you react to that hymn? Would its newness become so overwhelming that the words were unheard? Would its tricky tune quickly end your attempts at singing? Or, would the very fact of its newness focus your attention upon it! Could God use the new tune and the new verse to speak to you?

> *Come back quickly to the Lord,*
> *just come back to the Lord.*
> *Our Lord waits every day*
> *with his doors kept open wide.*
> *He is anxiously waiting for you*
> *every day and every night.*

It was written during the Second World War by a Korean Christian, Young Taik Chun. It was translated into English by his granddaughter. I suspect that the Nazareth synagogue congregation would not have liked that intrusion into the so-familiar of the worship time.

We do back away from change. We even take offense at it, sometimes. There is a story floating around about a pastor who gave his annual give-up-something-for-Lent homily. He pastored a small church in the northern part of our country. Early March was a chilly time, if not down right cold! He ended his sermon saying, "As an example of penitence to the rest of the community, this congregation will worship in an unheated church for the whole of Lent!" As the parishioners made their way out into the damp, late winter chill, the pastor asked one of the members, "Ah, Mrs. James, and what have you decided to give up for Lent?" She replied, "Church!"

Yes, we can let the comfort of ordinary routines hide God's working in our midst. The warning is that we can miss something that may be for us life-saving!

The wonderment is that God does use the ordinary and routine to fulfill divine purposes. Consider your own life. Look at all the routines that fill the days and weeks. The getting up for work each day. The responsibilities of carting the kids around. The shopping and dish doing and grass cutting and letter writing. God works within the everyday activities to bless us, and to fulfill divine purposes.

Each February some newspaper or magazine reproduces an old cartoon drawing of two farmers talking over a split-rail fence. Off in the distance is a small log cabin, with chimney smoke trailing into the sky. There is a date written at the top of the drawing: 1809. One farmer says, "What's new out your way?" The reply, "Aw, nothing much, except that Tom and Nancy Lincoln had a little baby last week." We need the reminder: God uses the ordinary for his purposes.

The rejection of Jesus in Nazareth initiated the first missionary thrust. What had been one voice now was 12 plus one. What had been one healing touch now was 12 plus one. Further, we often think that God's work must be through such grand events as the sun standing still, or the Red Sea being pushed aside. That may be, but much more God works in the ordinary, the routine, the undramatic.

Red Skelton told this story from the stage of the Palladium in London. He said there was a terrible flood in Louisiana. The water rose so quickly that a man had no time to escape and climbed to the roof of his house. As he perched on the house top and as the waters reached his ankles, a man in a rowboat came by. "Can I help you?" he shouted from the boat. "No," said the man, "the Lord will take care of me." Soon the water was at his waist. A second boat came by. Again the offer of help. Again the reply, "No, the Lord will take care of me." Not long after that, the water had risen to his neck. A helicopter whirled into view. The stranded man shouted, "Go on. God will take care of me." Well, he drowned and went to heaven. Once through the pearly gates he asked the Lord, "I've been faithful. What happened? Why didn't you save me?" The Lord replied, "Well, I really don't know what happened. I sent two rowboats and a helicopter!"

That is a funny story, but it translates into some very unfunny realities about God's saving work through the ordinary.

At a meeting of a children's home board, mention was made of how the home was helping a little, unnamed child cope with the severe sexual abuse he had been subjected to by his parents. How very, very sad are the reports of child abuse by parents. Some parents cover their abuse, thinking of it in religious terms! You and I understand that the routine, ordinary, humdrum activity of being a parent should be the arena in which God is at work for the good nurturing of children! Your role as a parent, a grandparent, is doing the work of God! The nurture you provide is part of the working of God. That divine nurturing consists of the simple, ordinary human qualities of love and encouragement and steadfastness and interest. Almost anyone can provide it, sensing that God is at work in the ordinary and the routine. From those ordinary human characteristics, through that children's home, God is mending that little eight-year-old child. Ten billion dollars could not replace the ordinary tasks of human caring and love. I wonder how many other children are abused because of parents who do not provide the ordinary, simple gifts of love, attention, encouragement and steadfastness.

The wonderment is that God can use us in the midst of the routines of every day. God can mend and heal and make whole lives right in the midst of ordinary circumstances. And thus we are part of that extension begun by Jesus when he sent out his disciples two by two. You and I are part of that company that speaks of God's love for us and for all his children.

The warning: We can miss God at work in our midst when we cling so unthinkingly to old and hard routines. The wonderment: God does continue to work his way in our midst through those ordinary routines. Where is the Lord God speaking to you through the routines of your living, through the ordinary? Samuel and Eli, and that synagogue in Nazareth, did not understand. Let us not walk in their shoes! Instead, "Come, let us walk in the way of the Lord." Amen!

Ordinary Time 15
Mark 6:7-13

A Solitary Witness

The raw skin on Marcus' ankle was still bleeding as he began work in Herod's palace. Never mind that the chains had rubbed raw the young skin. Never mind that the healing would take time, and would leave a life-long scar. Never mind that the cut, extending clear around his ankle, hurt with each step. Marcus was a slave. One did not have such concerns about slaves. They were expendable, like the clay tablets that the money counters used.

And, even if someone did care about the new slave, there were much more important things to think about. Herod's palace had been in an uproar since the jailing of the preacher, John. Nothing, it seemed, would silence this Jewish preacher. His wild dress drew the crowds, and his condemnation of Herod had become quite fashionable. And so, with slave chains, he was put into the prison of the palace. There he languished until one evening when young Marcus was called upon to bring the severed head of the preacher into the very presence of Herod! Marcus had seen much brutality in his young life. He was very familiar with violent death. But this gruesome task was beyond anything he had experienced.

Herod was drunk. His dinner party had long since become a shouting match between himself and his wife. As reported in the slave quarters, the great king had made a promise to his wife's daughter — a promise he had to keep. It was thought he wanted to retreat from it, but he had spoken the words. Once the words were spoken he could not take them back. Others had heard. And so Marcus the slave, with bleeding ankle, carried the head of John the Baptist into the presence of the king. It was a terrible moment, a moment that Marcus remembered all his days.

It can be a terrible thing to be held by the words of a promise.

Or it can be a wonderful thing!

This very familiar scripture story of King Herod's promise becomes a negative text from which a positive message may grow! I center our thought on verse 26 of the text. Herod made a promise in front of his family, his peers, his court. In his perceived position, in his arrogance, he discovered that he must hold to his promise. The words had been spoken. Because of those words, John the Baptist was beheaded.

Now verse 26 also speaks of another sort of word spoken. The Christian's commitment to Jesus Christ is a promise. Sometimes it is made before our family and peers. Always it is a promise made before God! The steadfastness of that promise is a very wonderful thing. It is like living water. It is like a house built on a rock. It is like putting on the whole armor of God.

But let another story tell of the power of the promise. This one is a true story.

St. Radegund is a very tiny village in Austria, edged against the German borderland. It is hard to find. It is not on many maps. It is so small there is no post office in St. Radegund. In that little village there is a tiny church, perched high over the river dividing Germany and Austria. Next to that tiny church is a graveyard. Within the grounds is a grave holding the ashes of a farmer. He was a very simple man. His life was undistinguished as the world seems to judge lives, except that in 1943 that peasant farmer, a father of three little children, was taken away to die in Berlin. There is a wooden cross over the grave and upon the cross is the name, Franz Jagerstatter.

Franz Jagerstatter was born in 1907. He was a farmer. He had no schooling beyond the fifth grade. His father was killed in a battle of the First World War. Franz grew up as a very average youth. He had a loud motorcycle of which he was very proud. He was once fined for his involvement in a fistfight with a group of youth from a neighboring village. It may be that he fathered a child out of wedlock, as he himself was born out of wedlock.

His friends and neighbors were surprised to learn that Franz, in his early 20s, enrolled in voluntary religious classes conducted by the pastor of St. Radegund. By the end of that decade of his life a change had occurred. It was a change that those close to him said was "sudden and total." "It was," said a neighbor, "as if he had been possessed by a higher power." Now he never passed a church without stopping in for meditation. Now he was sometimes noticed interrupting his labor in the field in order to pray. For a time he thought about joining a religious community, but ultimately he decided in favor of family life and farming. He married in 1936. He and his bride honeymooned with a trip to Rome. The children arrived: three little girls.

With his religious awakening came a deepened social concern. He saw the essential godlessness of the growing Nazi movement. His praying grew longer and more intense. In 1938, when Austrians voted in favor of national annexation with Nazi Germany, Franz resisted. He spoke out against the plan. He received pressure from the pastor, the mayor and many neighbors. "Don't call attention to our village," he was warned by all, "for our voting can change nothing." Still, he cast the village's only dissenting vote.

In the summer of that same year he had a remarkable dream. His words described it: "I saw a beautiful, shining railroad train that circled around a mountain. Streams of children, and adults as well, rushed toward the train and could not be held back." In his dream he heard a voice say the train was going to hell. It became clear in his mind that the train was Nazism; that he and every citizen of that Third Reich were among the passengers. He had to make a choice between his religious faith and the political order. To choose his faith would require a means of resistance. "I would like to call out to everyone," he wrote in his journal, "jump out of the train before it reaches its destination, even if it costs your life!"

Like every able-bodied Austrian man, Jagerstatter was called to military service. His draft notice arrived in February 1943. His oldest daughter was five. He sought spiritual counsel. "What does God want me to do?" Here was, for him, a meeting of the spirit world and the temporal world. Ignoring the advice of his pastor and many others, he refused to take the military oath. His promise had been to Someone else. For this he was immediately jailed. He was offered noncombatant service. He refused. It would still mean that he must wear the uniform.

In pencil on the pages of an ordinary composition book he asked himself, "For what purpose, then, did God endow all men with reason and free will if, in spite of this, we are obliged to render blind obedience?" And, he wrote some letters from his prison cell. "Just as the one who thinks only of this world does everything possible to make life here easier and better, so must we too, who believe in the eternal kingdom, risk everything in order to receive a great reward there."

He wrote: "The surest mark [of the follower of Jesus] is found in deeds showing love of neighbor. To do to one's neighbor what one would desire for oneself is more than merely not doing to others what one would not want done to oneself. Let us love our enemies, bless those who curse us, pray for those who persecute us. For love will conquer and endure for eternity. And happy are they who live and die in God's love."

This was practiced, even in the prison cell. The prison chaplain in Berlin (Dean Kreuzberg) said later, "I can say with certainty that this simple man is the only saint I have ever met in my lifetime."

On June 6, 1943, Franz Jagerstatter was found guilty of "undermining the military power" and sentenced to death. New attempts were made to save his life. His wife and the young priest who had replaced his exiled pastor journeyed to Berlin to see him. As they talked with him, they could see traces of the hunger and abuse he was undergoing. They talked of "duty," of "only following orders," of the state's "authority," of the fact that his solitary actions would ultimately mean nothing. He replied that he did not wish to be guilty of any injustice, he could not take even the slightest part in it. They left the prison and Berlin with the assurance that he was happy to have come so far without weakening, and that he was confident he could continue so to the end.

The court's sentence was fulfilled. Franz Jagerstatter was beheaded. He was not yet 37 years old. The date was August 9, 1944. Just before his death, he wrote, "I am convinced that it is best that I speak the truth even if it costs me my life."

A few people called him a martyr. In 1987 a memorial mass was conducted in Linz, Austria, culminating a three-day observance that would have been his 80th birthday. Other people have called him a deserter. They cited his family responsibilities. They said his act became a condemnation upon all those who did not express a conscientious objection. Still other people saw it only as a senseless waste of human life.

Historian Reinhold Schneider wrote: "When the commission of sin [intersects] one's sacred duty, there remains nothing else to do but to refuse and thus to bear witness, even solitary witness. But where such witness is, there is the kingdom of God!"

Each one of us is involved in "solitary witness." It is because of a promise made, perhaps in front of friends and family, but always before God. The promise and the witness will not take us to the beheading block. But it will determine our course in life. Franz Jagerstatter saw his life as more than being a peasant farmer from St. Radegund. He saw his life as more than a span of years upon earth. In that vision he touched the core of religion. Of course, martyrs are made from such stuff. But so are you and I! That is the message of promises to be kept, even from such a person as King Herod!

Ordinary Time 16
Mark 6:30-34

The Compassionate Highway

Her name was Mary. Quite a common name. She lived in a village near Capernaum, a village of fishermen who worked Lake Galilee through the night hours. Mary was childless and unmarried. She was cared for by her older brother, who was more like her father in that he was twice her age. She was 18. Her brother was 36 although ages were not kept in that ancient day nor in that little village. Her brother was simply one of the elders, an old man. And Mary was the sister that he must care for. She was a sweet person, kind and loving. And pretty, too. Also, she was a cripple. One leg was shorter than the other and so she did not walk very much, which meant that she was fatter than most 18-year-olds. She had so little exercise. Sometimes she would walk short distances, but it was difficult for her. Therefore she just sat and talked with those who walked by. Her name was Mary. Quite a common name. And that is about it! Except that one day her brother carried her on his back all the way to the next village. And there, on a bright spring afternoon, Jesus touched her leg and, looking intently into her eyes, said, "Mary, you can walk!" Later that afternoon, that wonderful afternoon, Mary walked back to her own village. She walked slowly, and with some pain, but she was not carried by her brother. She walked, and her life was never again as it had been!

That is a make-believe story. Still, I ask you to remember Mary, for she is really us! Our name is Mary.

Two bits of the gospel story are put together for today's lectionary lesson from Mark. First (6:30-34), the disciples have been out in the neighborhood, teaching the words that Jesus had taught them and doing the good deeds that they had seen him do. You remember that, after his rejection in Nazareth, he commissioned his close followers to be his messengers to the world. Now they have returned to Jesus with reports of their work. I suppose we might even say, in today's images, that the sales force is back at general headquarters. The calls have been made. The results are being tallied. But, unlike some of today's images, Jesus is deeply aware of the emotional drain upon his friends. It must have been evident to Jesus that the disciples had traveled far, had been diligent in their teaching, and had given unstintingly of themselves in their healing of life's hurts. Now, together again, Jesus says it is time for rest, time to recharge the batteries!

Dr. William Barclay, in his commentary on this part of Mark, says that these words of scripture describe "the rhythm of the Christian life." It is not possible to be all that Christ asks us to be without moments of retreat and renewal. It is not possible to be all of the time at the tasks of feeding the hungry and healing the ill and clothing the naked and comforting the dying — without stepping back into times of renewing our resources. Burnout can happen to church workers as well as to those in the teaching profession or in sales. Occasionally I worry about some folks who are the good deed doers in local churches. They assume so many worthy responsibilities and carry out the tasks so conscientiously that there may come the day when they must back away to restore their resources. If they do not, they can break! That break does not serve the Master's purpose, nor build his kingdom.

Jesus proposed that spiritual restoring by trying to take a boat to the other side of the Galilee Lake. He and his disciples were headed for a lonely place. That is not only an ancient practice. I have a friend in ministry who annually goes to a Roman Catholic monastery in another state for such retreat. There he has a room, a cot, a chair and desk and the chapel bells that sound every three hours, inviting him to times of thoughtful meditation. In that place, he is separated from the intensity of his daily work. From that place, alone he is resourced to better enter the intensity of ministry once again. Also, I found the high mountains of Colorado to be such a time for me. It is helpful for more than priests and ministers! It is the sort of help provided to a young mother by a mother's morning out. It is the sort of help provided by going to a ball game, or, I am told by someone close to me, by going shopping at the mall! We do need that rhythm in our lives that backs us away from the pressure and allows us the time apart for strength-gaining.

Of course, the most obvious (and least understood) time for such spiritual strength-gaining is what we are about at this hour! We come to the sanctuary, the sacred place set apart, in order that we might be blessed, forgiven, recharged for the opportunities of ministry that call to all of us when we leave this place. One old Colonial church had upon its front door's lintel, on the outside, the words, "Come to worship God." The same lintel, on the inside, said, "Leave to serve God's children." Both directions are necessary. I find that so in my life. I hope you do, too! Poet Mary Hallet knew this when she wrote:

> *Until I caught the rhythm of [Christ's] life,*
> *I had not heard the music of the spheres,*
> *The simple cadences of ancient psalms,*
> *The lyric beauty of a thousand years.*

Yet, even as Jesus and the disciples sought the solitude, that sanctuary on the other side of the lake, the plight of the crowd was very evident. You can picture it geographically. Jesus and the disciples left the people at one point on the Galilee shoreline. They took the boat across, but the people saw the direction they were sailing. They followed the boat, running along the shoreline. With little wind upon the sea to speed the boat, the crowds met the tired Jesus and the tired disciples as their boat was beached upon the far shore.

What should they do? What would you do? This scripture gives a wonderful little window into Jesus' psyche. Despite the need for rest, he is "moved to the depths of his being with pity for them." Those are Mark's words. There was such compassion about Jesus. The image is of a shepherd sensing his responsibility for the sheep. The crowds that again clustered around were "like sheep who had no shepherd." And so Jesus again began to talk with them, and to share with them the wholeness of God's love and acceptance that would make them complete. His teaching was of their worth in God's sight and that the power of worth gave them strength to live. Jesus gave of himself, still. Sometimes the rhythm of life is interrupted. The desired and necessary rest is once again pushed aside in order that the task of caring take place. That is the message of verses 30-34.

The lectionary text for this day jumps over two major events in Jesus' ministry, as recorded in Mark's sixth chapter. Next is the little boy's gift of five loaves and two fish that feed the multitude (Mark 6:35-44) and then is the story of Jesus' solitude in prayer that ended with his meeting the disciples, "walking on the sea." (Mark 6:45-52) These two texts are proposed for later study, so that today's scripture reading concludes with the general word about the crowds coming to Jesus for healing. Their faith was so strong that some begged "to be allowed to touch even the tassel of his robe; and all who touched it were restored to health." Those are Mark's words. Such was the faith in God's power through Jesus that even to touch the little prayer shawl tassel would bring healing.

We do not need to understand, with our scientific mind set, all the ways by which healing took place 2,000 years ago. If a broken life is made whole, it is a miracle whether it followed the science of psychology and medicine or was by an act of interrupting all the laws of nature! Blindness can be caused by acid thrown upon the eyes or by shellshock upon the mind. But the curing of blindness, no matter what the cause, is a miracle — then and now! The crippled limp is caused by the accidental crushing of bones or by some deep psychic trauma. But the curing of a crippled leg is a miracle — then and now. A body declared dead, whether from a heart stopped or a fevered coma, and then restored to life is miracle enough for any age. A life rejected and scorned and spit upon and told "you ain't worth nothing," is brought to wholeness with word of divine forgiveness and acceptance. That is a miracle whether on the Galilee shoreline or in the suburbs!

You see, we are that crowd that ran around the edge of the sea. We still come to Jesus for healing. We want only to reach out to him in spirit-touch. We still seek him that we might be forgiven for the sins we have done. In that forgiveness we can be healed. We seek him to confess the evil we have condoned. That confession, too, brings healing. We desire that the emotional burden we bear might be lifted from us — or shared. To share such a burden with Christ is to find healing. And, in his companionship, we can discover a wholeness that replaces the brokenness that is part of our life. Such discovery brings healing! His word upon the shoreline is the same word he speaks today. And the result is the same, for we, too, so often live as sheep without a shepherd!

> *We would see Jesus! We would look upon*
> *The light in that divinely human face,*
> *Where lofty majesty and tender grace*
> *In blended beauty shone.*
>
> *We would see Jesus, and would hear again*
> *The voice that charmed the thousands by the sea,*
> *Spoke peace to sinners, set the captives free,*
> *And eased the sufferers' pain.*

*We would see Jesus, yet not him alone —
But see ourselves as in our Maker's plan;
And in the beauty of the Son of Man
See man upon his throne.*

*We would see Jesus, and let him impart
The truth he came among us to reveal,
Till in the gracious message we should feel
The beating of God's heart. Amen.*

— W. J. Suckow

Assayings: Theological Faith Testings

Robert L. Salzgeber

Ordinary Time 17
John 6:1-5

Sarah And
The WECON Council

"A large crowd followed (Jesus), because they had seen his miracles of healing the sick." Notice the crowd's condition for following Jesus. There is an angel. He was able to heal sick people, therefore they followed. There was one more reason why Jesus would have been somewhat reticent about openly sharing miracles, signs and wonders. He did not wish people to follow him simply because he was able to physically heal people. Others could do that also. So he would often ask his followers to tell no one about the miracles he had done.

The point is that Jesus already knew himself to be the Son of the living God. He did not have to prove anything. When he healed people he was genuinely giving gifts; giving of himself. There were no angels as far as he was concerned. He simply desired the people to know who he really was. He wanted them to know that he was not just some physical healer among many, but Jesus, the Christ, the humble servant revealer of God. No conditions were needed to qualify for Jesus' life-giving water. Jesus simply desired to know two things. First, did the person really want to be healed? Jesus realized that many people do not want to change and grow. Thus, they do not desire spiritual healing. Two, why me? And if the person saw in Jesus, God desiring to be that person's friend and savior, Jesus would offer himself as healer. He would freely offer spiritual food. No conditions. No angels.

So when Jesus asked Philip, "Where can we buy enough food to feed all these people?" quite naturally, Jesus was simply testing Philip because he already knew what he would do. Of course he knew what he would do. He was God. Jesus wanted to see if Philip trusted his kingship, his sovereignty.

And then Andrew said, "There is a boy here who has five loaves of barley bread and two fish. But they will certainly not be enough for all these people." And a little child fed them! There were even 12 baskets left over. This is the extent of Jesus' power and kingship.

Seeing the miracle that Jesus had performed, the people wanted to seize him in order to make him king by force. This is the point of the text, the point of the people's misunderstanding. Make Jesus king by force? Actually seize him and force him to be king? How absurd. He already was king. He rules however, not from a throne but from a cross. This is the extent of the multitudes' misunderstanding of the kingdom. So Jesus went off to the hills by himself.

Because Jesus is already king he is able to feed the following crowd that has gathered. Because Jesus is already king, the Son of God, he also empowers us, his church, to feed the masses of hungry people in the world. The resources are present. The question is, are we willing to count the cost and pay the price? Are we willing to let go of established traditions and ways of doing things and change and grow and sacrifice and even suffer on behalf of the hungry and malnourished? Or do we not desire to be spiritually healed by Jesus? That is why Jesus asked a potential follower, "Do you desire to be healed?" He asks us the same question. "Do you desire to be healed? Do you desire to be my friend? Do you see God in me? If so, come join me in my kingdom work. Let's feed the world together."

Jesus is king and desires the world to be fed with his spirit and truth. It is the selfish world which resists his kingship. Jesus is already king. He doesn't need to be seized and made king by force. And that is exactly what our sin is. We have told Jesus that we want him to rule and solve the problems of the world our way, not his way. We desire our brand of peace, not his way of peace.

A parable: The air was heavy with seriousness and Sarah faced the gathered WECON council. Realizing that this was not just a normal, regular meeting, the atmosphere in the council chamber was gloomy and dismal. There was a somberness in Sarah's voice. As chairperson of this austere group she called the meeting of the World Ecclesiastical Council Of Nations to order at exactly the appointed time.

With the echo of her gavel still ricocheting off the paneled walls of the large meeting room Sarah spoke determinedly, "Thank you all for coming on such short notice. I know the distances are quite great for many of you. I realize it is also difficult to get flight reservations into Geneva at the last minute. It is good to see you. May God bless you and may our Lord be with us today in our deliberations. So, why are we here? As you know, many nations during the last decade have converted their large defense budgets toward the economic preservation and assistance of poor nations. But unfortunately, the tractors and plows of the rich can do as much harm as their swords. Modern expensive trucks can do more lasting damage than military tanks. Put very simply my friends, the rich of the world are getting richer and the poor are getting poorer. And the poor and hungry are increasing daily. How shall we feed them? Unfortunately, we have forgotten how to talk about modern transportation that does not rely on fast cars and airplanes. Our ideas of modern health care only lift up our ability to prolong the lives of the desperately ill. We think of better education only in terms of more complex schools and teachers who possess more and more degrees. Huge industries and institutions manufacturing and producing costly products and services, which the poor cannot afford, dominate our developing nations. The poor are going hungry while their wealthy exporter agri-business neighbor plows away on his modern tractor next door."

Sarah looked over at Daniel who was kind of impetuous and always claimed he knew all the answers. "Well, Daniel, how are we going to feed the hungry multitudes of the world?" (She asked Daniel this to test him. Actually she already knew what the council must propose.)

Timidly, and without much confidence in his voice, Daniel spoke, "I don't know Sarah. The world situation is grave. In most developing countries, the population grows, and so does the middle class. But the gap between the middle class and the poor and hungry masses is ever widening. The majority of people have less food now than in 1945. And if that wasn't bad enough, there exists less actual care of the sick, less meaningful work, and less protection in the form of shelter and housing. Part of this is due to the breakdown of the traditional family and culture but much of it is caused by the production of products which only the privileged can afford. Today, more people suffer from hunger, pain and exposure than they did at the end of World War II, not only in numbers, but also as a percentage of the world population. I'm sorry Sarah, but unfortunately I don't have an answer for you this time."

"Thank you Daniel," Sarah said. "The issue is complicated. The problem is "package deals." So long as every person "needs" his car, our cities must endure longer traffic jams and absurdly expensive remedies to relieve them. As long as health means maximum length of survival, our sick will get ever more extraordinary surgical inventions and drugs required to deaden their resulting pain. As long as we desire to use school to get children out of their parent's hair or to keep them off the streets and out of the labor force, our young will be retained in endless schooling and will need ever-increasing premiums and incentives to endure the ordeal. Phillip, I see you are anxious to speak."

"Thank you Sarah. You are certainly right about packaged solutions. The needs of the world's poor have been converted to the demand for new brands and "package deals" which, for the majority of them, are forever beyond their reach. This is what I would call underdevelopment. This happens even in poor countries where the supply of classrooms, food, cars and doctors is rising. Why? Because those in power build up services and products which have been designed for the middle class and wealthy. Once they have monopolized demand, including the demand of the poor, they can never satisfy the poor majorities' needs because the poor majority will never be able to afford the high cost. So unfortunately, real needs have been turned into the demand for manufactured products. What I mean is that thirst has been translated into the needs for cola."

"I know exactly what you are saying Phillip. Thanks so much for your insight. I know of underdeveloped doctors who get training at New York hospitals for special surgery, which they apply to only a few back home. Meanwhile amoebic dysentery remains endemic in slums where 90 percent of the population lives."

Joseph spoke up, "That's the issue right here. Each car which an underdeveloped nation puts on the road denies 50 people good transportation by bus. Each merchandised refrigerator reduces the chance of building a community freezer. Every dollar spent on doctors and hospitals costs a hundred lives. If each dollar was spent on providing safe drinking water, a hundred lives could have been saved. Each dollar spent on schooling means more privileges for the few at the cost of the many. It increases the number of those who, before dropping out, have been taught that those who stay longer have earned the right to more power, wealth and prestige. I'm not talking against education here. We need more and better education. I'm talking about school. What schooling does is to teach the schooled the superiority of the better schooled."

"Thank you for your thoughts, Joseph," said Sarah. "In an underdeveloped country elementary school attendance certainly does harness the worker to the boss. The seventh-grade dropout feels his inferiority much more than the dropout from the third grade. Why? Because the school dropout is held personally responsible for his or her failure. This failure breeds the notion that it is impossible to live without being inferior to others. Some underdeveloped countries have even already passed laws doubling the years during which schooling is legally compulsory and free. From now on those who drop out under the age of 16 will be faced during their lifetime with the reproach that he or she did not take advantage of this legally obligatory privilege. Fine and dandy, but unfortunately laws such as this are passed in countries where even the most optimistic could forsee the day when such levels of schooling would be provided for only 25 percent of the young. These children, when they drop out, are condemned to marginality and exclusion from social life, in short, underdevelopment and hunger." Sarah saw that the entire assembly was looking at her for direction. Sarah boldly spoke, her words were direct, "Just think of the multiple uses for a simple can opener, whereas an electric one, if it works at all, opens only some kinds of cans and costs 100 times as much. Affluent farmers can become convinced of their need for a four-axle vehicle which can go 70 miles per hour on the highways, has an electric windshield wiper and upholstered seats, and can be turned in for a new one within a year or two. Most of the world's farmers don't need such speed, nor are they interested in obsolescent consumerism. They need low-cost transportation in a world where time is not money, where manual wipers suffice, and where a piece of heavy equipment should outlast a generation. This vehicle is not being produced by any manufacturer in the world at the present time. Most developing nations need para-medical workers who can function for indefinite periods without the supervision of an M.D. Instead of establishing a process to train midwives and visiting healers who know how to use a very limited arsenal of medicines while working independently, poor and hungry governments establish every year a new school of specialized nursing or nursing administration to prepare professionals who can function only in a hospital."

Daniel's eyes began to brighten and his posture perked up, "You are absolutely right, Sarah! That's the solution. Money is now spent largely on children, but an adult can be taught to read in one tenth the time and for one-tenth the cost it takes to teach a child. And in the case of an adult there is an immediate return on the investment, such as new insight, political awareness, the willingness to assume responsibility for his family's size and future, or increased productivity. There is even a double return in the case of the adult. Not only can he or she contribute to the education of his children, but to that of other adults as well. But too often literacy programs are pushed aside in developing nations where schools have first call on all public resources."

"I'm reading you loud and clear, Daniel," said Philip. "Even the basic supply of books, pictures, blocks, games and toys are totally absent from the homes of the really poor. These same educational items enable a middle-class child to learn the alphabet, the colors, shapes and other classes of objects and experiences which insure his or her educational progress."

"I have in mind a different kind of solution which has been largely neglected up to now as you have noted by our conversation," said Sarah. "We must call for research on alternatives to the packaged products which now dominate the market; to hospitals and the profession dedicated to keeping the terminally ill alive; to schools and the packaging process which refuses education to those who are not of the right age. A disclaimer is in order. I am not against compassion for the ill and dying. But I am advocating compassion for all who are hungry and ill and dying. Thousands of young and potentially healthy and productive people die each day because of poor drinking water, something that we take entirely for granted.

"Underdevelopment is the result of rising levels of aspiration achieved through the intensive marketing of patent, privileged products. The hungry masses of the world need to be given the spiritual gift and food of awakening awareness of new levels of God-given potential and the use of one's God-given creative powers to foster human life. Underdevelopment, however, implies the surrender of social consciousness to pre-packaged solutions. The only way to reverse this disastrous trend to increasing underdevelopment and hunger is to learn to laugh at accepted solutions in order to change the demand which make them necessary. Only people made free by God's love can change their minds and be surprised."

I am indebted to Ivan D. Illich's provocative thought in his book *Celebration of Awareness*, Doubleday & Company, Inc., 1970, for the dialogue in the above parable.

Ordinary Time 18
John 6:24-35

Charlie Used To Do That

The people said, "Our ancestors ate manna in the desert, just as the scripture says, 'He gave them bread from heaven to eat.' " Jesus answered, "What Moses gave you was not the bread from heaven; it is my Father who gives you the real bread from heaven."

Jesus is referring to the fact that even when God gave the whole Israelite community manna the people still complained; they were not satisfied. God then gave the Hebrews quail and they continued to be dissatisfied. Later on the whole Israelite community complained to Moses and said, "Give us water to drink." Moses struck a rock and water came out of it for people to drink. But the whole Israelite community continued not to be satisfied. They continued to hunger and thirst after righteousness.

"I am the bread of life," Jesus told them. "He who comes to me will never be hungry; he who believes in me will never be thirsty."

Jesus is once again making reference to a common everyday thing in order to say something about the kingdom of his Father. Jesus uses bread in his little object lesson. There were two kinds of bread: good bread and bad bread; the bread of life and the bread of un-life. Today, in our culture, people who raise livestock know the importance of good nutrition for their animals, not for themselves. Ironically, the intelligent farmer orders the best possible diet for his pigs, which he raises to die, while he feeds white bread to his children, whom he raises, presumably to live. Why? Because there is a large profitable animal feed market for the bran and the wheat germ which the miller gets free. The best part of the grain of wheat is stolen before it ever gets to us and is poured into animals to make them healthier than children.

In Jesus' day the farmers did not know this yet. So they left the good stuff in their bread; the bran and the wheat germ. This is the part of the bread that spoils quickly, turning rancid and moldy. This kind of bread couldn't be kept without a great deal of preservatives, like white bread can be kept today. A loaf of white bread will keep in my refrigerator for well over a week. But in Jesus' day, and continuing even today in the Middle East, bread had to be baked fresh every morning. And if not eaten that same day, by nightfall the same bread would be hard, stale and the mold and fungus of decay would be already beginning its work. This was the bread of un-life which Jesus would have been thinking about as he told his hearers about himself being the bread of life. The bread of life would have been the fresh smelling newly baked bread of the morning dawn. This is what Jesus was. "I am the bread of life," Jesus told them. Jesus was referring to himself as the bread which would be everlastingly fresh. He was comparing his kingdom with a never ending dawn's early light where the aroma of fresh baked bread would fill the people so that they would never be hungry again. This bread, Jesus was saying, would have the preservative of the Father's kingdom.

What is this bread of life like then? Since in Aramaic one of the meanings of Satan or evil is distortion, the bread of life would be able to discern truth as opposed to falsehood. Thus, the preservative of the kingdom would be to preserve the people from illusion. The bread of life then, would be to not let the people become separated from the reality and love of God. The bread of life would be to know that the bread of un-life, the bread of death, Satan himself, this illusion, can really have no lasting effect upon us. That is if we continue to eat the bread of life. In a sense, Jesus is saying here that if we partake of the bread of un-life, of death and illusion, we will become part of that very death and illusion. We will become partners with it and therefore co-inflictors of it. So Jesus says, "Come to me, I am the bread of life, partake of me, and you will never be hungry ever again."

What does this bread of life look like? I will answer with two short stories:

It was the year 1917. The place was an Armenian hospital in Mezre. Day after day, Elizabeth Caraman, a nurse in that hospital, cleansed and bound up the wounds of Turkish soldiers who had been wounded on the battlefields. Often when the soldiers came to her, hastily applied bandages were dried on to a gaping wound. It was extremely painful to remove them.

One day Elizabeth was working on an especially bad wound. To help the young soldier think about something besides the pain, she told him a little about her own history. "My father and I were deported from our home by the Turks," she said bitterly, "and my father was thrown into prison. In 1915 they took him out of his cell, rolled him in a carpet and hoisted him up on a donkey. Together with other Armenian men they sent him away to die." At this moment, Elizabeth, for some reason, looked up. To her surprise the young soldier was staring at her with a look of horror in his black eyes.

"What is the matter?" Elizabeth asked.

"I killed your father," he said in a low voice. Elizabeth could only gasp. With a super human effort, she went on cleansing the wound. "I rolled him off the donkey onto the ground," the soldier continued. "With one jab of the bayonet I killed him. I have never been able to forget it. The whole business of killing has sickened me."

Elizabeth felt a wave of hatred and sorrow sweep over her. Here was the murderer of her father. In some strange way, the enemy had fallen into her hands. She had the power to destroy him. At this moment Elizabeth thought of her mother.

What would she have done? Her mother loved Christ and tried to follow him. She would have tried to help this young man. The power and light of her mother's life reached out to Elizabeth.

Gently Elizabeth turned to the soldier lying in front of her. "Christ says we must forgive our enemies. For his sake, I forgive you." she said. The soldier stared at her in amazement. He could not say anything. Every day, when Elizabeth came to his bed to dress his wound, she saw him looking at her with awe and wonder in his eyes.

Finally, one day, he said to Elizabeth, "Your Christ must be very great! He surely is the bread of life. His teachings really live in your heart, for I see them in your life."

How glad Elizabeth was that God had given her the power to forgive her enemy! It cleansed all bitterness from her soul. Now she was free to love and live again.[1]

Charlie was a man who, beyond a shadow of a doubt, knew he was extremely blessed by God. He had a loving wife who stood by him in both good times and bad times. He had four beautiful daughters and two wonderful sons. One evening, on his way home from the furniture store at which he worked, he thought about how hard they had all worked in building the house on Brady Street which they had moved into the previous year. "Yes," he considered, "my family and I are certainly blessed of God!"

Every day on his way home from work Charlie would take a kind of inventory of things that needed to be done as he walked past the church where he had been a member since his baptism in 1917. Whenever he was at the church he would notice things that needed to be done. Sometimes they were just little things like changing a light bulb. On his way home from working at the furniture store all day, if there was something that needed fixing, Charlie patiently climbed the church steps and went to work at the task at hand.

Sometimes it was marks on the tile floor scuffed by the children's playing. "Many people in the congregation wouldn't agree with me," Charlie thought, as he began to remove the scuff marks with lots of elbow grease, "but I love these marks made by the children. Oh my, what would the kingdom be like without the energy and aliveness of kids?"

On other days it would be light bulbs that Charlie would stop and take time to replace. Consider, he would, the light of Christ as he moved throughout the church with his ladder. On another day he remembered that the previous Sunday he had noticed a leaky faucet that needed new washers. As he checked out the spigot he remembered the life-giving water of his baptism. Sometimes squeaky doors had to be oiled and he would go around to every door and oil the hinges and latches so that they worked properly. While doing this he would recall that Jesus was the door to life. That Christ was the threshold to the kingdom of God. The next day it would be windows. One day he would clean the outside. The next day he would clean the inside of the windows. And the next day he would check and oil the latches and sand and revarnish any bare wood that he saw. As he looked through each window he would think, "It is only with the heart of the kingdom that one can see rightly, what is essential is invisible to the naked eye."

Then there was always the furnace in the hall. Charlie replaced the filters and made sure that the pilot light was on. And he would be reminded of the love and warmth of God's Son, Jesus. On hot summer days he would often fix screens and while doing so reflect on the cool breeze of God's mercy. There were always wastebaskets that needed to be emptied and trash that needed to be carried out for the garbage man to pick up. And Charlie would consider humanity's garbage, sin, the dark side. The next day when he would be cleaning the dirty oven he would in turn rejoice in the reality that God redeems his children from their sin and darkness to newness of life.

Charlie was certainly a man blessed of God. He was blessed in knowing God's Son, the bread of life. Charlie lived a long rich life. When he was 87 years old he slipped on the ice while walking up his front steps one evening having been at the church to fix a leaky commode. He never returned home after that. When he left the hospital he went to live at a nearby nursing home where he received the best of care.

And for a long time after that members of the church where Charlie went would say things like, "Look at those marks on the floor, why aren't they being cleaned up? I cannot see to sing or read in church. The lights above me are burned out. Why doesn't someone fix those darned doors that squeak so loud when you come into the church? Why is it so cold in here? You mean to tell me that someone didn't get the furnace ready for winter?" And at least one person always seemed to be standing nearby and would say, "Well, Charlie used to do that." Charlie died in 1987 at 94 years of age. People still ask things like, "How come these windows are so dirty?" There always seems to be at least one person who remembers and says, "Well, Charlie used to do that." Nobody ever really knew because Charlie always made sure that nobody was around when he did his little deeds. Accolades Charlie did not want. He only desired to work with Jesus in being the bread of life for others. And even today someone will come forward and say, "Well, Charlie used to do that."

---

[1]Adapted from the story "Could He Ever Be the Same Again?" in *Courage in Both Hands* by Allen A. Hunter (Fellowship of Reconciliation, 21 Audubon Ave., New York, 32, New York.)

Ordinary Time 19
John 6:41-51

The Robe

The people's question concerning "How Jesus said that he came down from heaven" was preconditioned by a particular Jewish mind-set of that day. The majority of the Hebrews, during the time of Jesus, believed that the spiritual world emanated from the physical world. Flesh, blood and race projected one's spiritual aura. So it is natural and normal for the people to grumble when Jesus says that he is the living bread that came down from heaven.

But Jesus taught that the physical being emanates from the spiritual realm. "And the spiritual Word became flesh and dwelt in the physical world." Jesus taught that the animated physical self is simply an extension of his Father's spiritual domain. Jesus promoted this idea, not to reduce that which is physical, but to help the people understand what is really important in life and what is of lesser importance; what is critical in life and what is simply window dressing; what is of a higher-priority reality and what is of a lower-priority nature; what is living bread which lasts forever and what is physical bread which begins to decay at the end of the day.

Because the tradition had become calcified over a period of many years, the people had become myopically stuck into thinking that God would never desire to be close to them. The tradition finally taught them to appease God through sacrifices, offerings and rituals. This was the only way that their physical natures could get close to God.

But Jesus tells the people to stop grumbling. He says that they are of his Father already, that no one can come to him unless the Father draws them to Jesus. Jesus is telling the people that they have come from the realm of God's spiritual world and so they should live as though they have already eaten the living bread from heaven. Implied here is that in Jesus people see and recognize who they really are as members of God's spiritual kingdom.

Recall the paragraph in the story of *The Ugly Duckling* when the ugly duck realizes who he really is. "He saw below him his own image, but he was no longer a clumsy dark grey bird, ugly and ungainly, he was himself a swan! It does not matter in the least having been born in a duck yard, if only you come out of a swan's egg!" Jesus was explaining to the gathered people that it was the same with them. It does not matter in the least having been from Nazareth and born in Bethlehem, if only you come out of the matrix and womb of God.

So Jesus proclaims that "Everyone will be taught by God." Because we have come out of the matrix of God we can claim our inheritance. We can claim the bread that comes down from heaven. The bread of such a kind that whoever eats it will not die. The bread that if anyone eats it, he/she will live forever. The bread is Jesus himself, which he gives so that the world may live. Thus Jesus invites us to consume him, to put him on, to wear him so that we will receive life.

A parable: Joshua scooted quickly out of the office building where he worked. As the elevator brought him down to the first floor of the glass and steel complex Josh couldn't wait to get over to The Hub. The Hub was an upscale men's clothing and fashion store in the heart of the city. Being only two blocks away from the entrance to Josh's office building, his one-hour lunch break afforded him just enough time to pick up a few things that he wanted.

As Josh walked into The Hub he said, "Hi David, how are you today?" David was the owner and operator of The Hub. He had taken a liking to Josh the first time he had walked into the store a year ago. He found Josh to be friendly and also a great customer.

"I'm just great, Josh. Tommy, my little boy, started to walk last night. Sarah and I are so excited. Boy, that Tommy is really something else. Do I love that little guy. What can I help you with today, Josh?"

"I saw a suit on someone the other day and I want to buy one with a similar cut. It even had a matching monogrammed shirt and tie," Josh said. "It's just like that one in the picture up there."

"Yes, Josh," said David, "We stock that particular ensemble but I must tell you that it is super expensive. I mean mega bucks. You sure you really want to spend that much?"

"Yeah, I think so," Josh said, "Let me try it on." So Josh took the suit into the dressing room. Several minutes later Josh came back out. "I can't possibly resist it, David. Wrap it up for me. The whole works. The suit, the shirt and the tie. I love it."

"Okay, Josh," said David as he rang up the sale. "With your good customer discount it comes to $398." As Josh handed David his credit card, David wondered what his credit limit was. David was beginning to worry a little about Josh. He was coming into the store several times a week now and his purchases were getting greater and greater. Josh didn't seem to be concerned about how much money he was spending though. He would just hand over one of his credit cards. David was beginning to think that maybe Josh was addicted to clothes. David liked clothes. "After all," he thought, "clothes are my business." But David had learned a long time ago that clothes certainly do not make the man.

"Sign right here Josh, and here is your receipt and your carbon. Enjoy your new suit, Josh!"

Moments later Josh was standing in the elevator waiting while it climbed the 25 floors to his office lobby. Josh thought about how much he loved his new suit but even in his vivacious and exuberant state there was a tinge of anxiety. He wasn't quite sure what his dread was all about. And then it kind of surfaced from his subconscious being. Josh remembered that some guy had called him from First National Bank early last evening telling him that if he did not make a $250 payment on his credit card the bank was going to shut off his credit. As he walked into his office he considered that both his major credit cards were pretty well maxed-out to the limit. "Yeah, I've really gotten carried away," Josh thought as he sat down at his desk and picked up a report in order to peruse it. Josh was only half into his work. "Boy, I've really become addicted to buying clothes. What is wrong with me anyway?"

But the next day Josh found himself once again standing in the middle of The Hub with his credit cards just burning holes in his pocket. Fortunately, he was the only one in the store and David noticed Josh's anxiety. He saw that Josh was flushed and kind of nervous. He thought that maybe Josh was getting sick.

"Are you all right Josh?" David questioned.

"Oh, I'm okay, David. Well, now that you ask I've got something that's really bugging me but I can't talk here. Can we get together some time and talk after work?"

"Sure Josh. How about over supper this evening at about 6 p.m. My relief clerk is coming in at five which means I will be free for the evening. Let's meet at the restaurant across the street at six."

"Okay, that sounds great. And David, thanks for taking the time to talk with me."

Six o'clock rolled around and Josh found himself sitting in a booth at the restaurant. He didn't have any idea how he would pay his credit cards off. "Life is boring and dull if you can't go out and buy stuff, especially clothes," Josh thought as he saw David walk through the glass door. David sat down across from Josh.

"Well, my good friend, what seems to be troubling you? You sure looked bleak at noon when I saw you. What can I do to help?"

Haltingly and embarrassingly Josh went on to explain to David about the credit cards and his addiction to wanting and buying more and more clothes. "A new suit makes me feel good for about two days and then I want to go out and buy another one," Josh explained to David. "You have an entire clothing store, David, and you seem to be happy!"

"Well, for one thing Josh, the clothing store is my business. If I took a suit out of the store every other day, I could not make a livelihood and provide for Sarah and Tommy. But you're right, I do have the opportunity to get a lot of clothes because of my buyer discounts. But I learned a long time ago that clothes and things can never finally make one happy and fulfilled. If you want to know the truth Josh, there is a garment that does ultimately bring me happiness. Do you want to know what the garment is?"

"David, I'd do anything right now to get myself on the right track."

"Well, I'll tell you if you promise not to laugh. Because some people think that it's ridiculous. But when I was baptized in my church many years ago, my pastor put a robe on me and said, 'Put on this robe, for in baptism you have been clothed in the righteousness of Christ, who calls you to his great feast of the bread of life.' That's it Josh. You may not believe me when I tell you this, but I only have two or three suits. Yes, I take home a fair amount of clothes but I give most of them away through my church's thrift shop. So now you know the secret of my joy. Would you like to find out more about the robe?"

"Yes, I think I would, David. But I'm not sure how that robe brings you so much joy."

"The robe is just a symbol. You see Josh, we are rich. The few societies which are well off are plagued by an emptiness never filled by frantic grasping for more and more stuff. We need to boldly walk into the darkness of human existence. There we face our sin and self-centeredness. In our darkness we meet the suffering God who bears the sin of the world. This God does not crush us. Rather, Josh, he forgives us and gives us the gift of salvation. A new direction. We join the crucified Christ in his unity with the pain of the world. So do you see why that robe is so important to me, Josh?"

"Yes, I'm really beginning to. I would really like to hear more, David. I can't believe that you own an entire clothing store and it hasn't eaten you right up! I know you have your problems, David, but you seem so able to handle them. You have a contentment that I desire. Do you think we could get together every week so that I could learn more about baptism and possibly put on one of those robes, too?"

"I'd love to meet with you regularly. But even better yet, I'm going to introduce you to my pastor so that he can teach you more about baptism. But remember friend, if you decide to get baptized, I get to put the robe on you, okay?"

"Okay, David, you're on!"

Ordinary Time 20
John 6:51-58

The Banquet

The people argued, "How can this man give us flesh to eat?" To eat and drink the Lord's portion of an offered sacrifice was considered (later on in the Jewish tradition) a desecration or offensive because it was believed that the sacrifice belonged to God. To consume the life force, to consume God, was believed to be a sacrilege.

But despite the religious calcification of the covenant tradition, the heart and spirit of the covenant tradition did break through at various times. One such time was when David ate the bread which was considered to be the Lord's portion and which only the priests were allowed to eat. (1 Samuel 21) Certain priests were consecrated and therefore held an exclusive right and holy privilege to eat the holy bread that was set apart for the temple sacrifice. Through this consuming of a very select few priests, God's hunger was believed to be satisfied.

Thus, the people listening to Jesus believed him to be showing contempt and a lack of reverence for God when he invited the people to eat his flesh; when he said that his flesh was the bread of life.

Last week we mentioned that the Jewish tradition, by the time of Jesus' ministry, finally evolved into believing that life, breath, wind, the life force all emanated from the physical sphere. From the domain of blood and flesh.

Thus, for the Hebrews, nationality, race, blood, the clan, the group, all became equated with life and salvation. One was saved by being a part of the right group, clan or race. One's blood line became very important. Salvation became equated with nepotism. One thought that by being related to Abraham one had automatically and ritually consumed the bread of life and salvation. Recall John's warning, "And don't think you can escape punishment by saying that Abraham is your ancestor. I tell you that God can take these rocks and make descendants for Abraham!" (Matthew 3:9)

Thus, the Hebrews believed they had to coax God with sacrificial offerings in order to get what they wanted from him. For the Jews, God was distant, hidden, not readily accessible. God did not associate intimately, so they thought. But this was actually an aberration of the original covenant as we see in today's lesson.

So the people had a strong need to lure God, to manipulate him, to appease and pacify him with exclusive sacrifice and ritual. God could never be close if it took this much work and currency to get his attention. And if it was this difficult to approach God, how could God ever be intimate with men and women?

For the Gentiles, the issue was just the opposite. Life and breath emanated from the spiritual realm. This is actually what John says, "And the Word became flesh and dwelt among us." But the Gentiles pushed this idea too far. They finally came to the conclusion that if all things emanated from the spirit world then the flesh was no good. One's spiritual life was then spent trying to get up and out and away from the flesh. They desired to get to God.

But this idea still made God distant and difficult to get to as well as approach. In this case one needed to possess the correct formula, steps, degrees, and assume the proper position and posturing in meditation, chants, rites, thoughts and prayers. All was said and done according to proper protocol so as not to offend the gods. All this in order to get to God!

But in our text, Jesus "tells it like it is," he comes clean with the people. He tells the people that they did not have to play ritualistic and posturing games to get his Father's attention. He says that his Father desires to be close to them. He says, "I am the living bread ... the bread I will give you is my flesh ... I give it so the world may live ... whoever eats my flesh and drinks my blood lives in me, and I live in him ... whoever eats me will live ..."

In order to make his point of how close his Father desires to be to the people Jesus says quite literally, "Eat me. Consume me. Put me on. Wear me. Take me into yourself. Participate with me in my Father's kingdom work. Lose yourself. Lose your life for my sake. Let go of established ways. Take me into yourself. Receive eternal life."

A story: Mark's schedule of late had been extremely busy and hectic. First, all of the area church cluster study meetings and the internal congregational long range study had resulted in enough extra meetings to send Mark reeling. And even now the intensity of his schedule continued. The results of all of the data recently collected was that the church where Mark was pastor was to undergo a complete and total renovation. This meant more time commitments, meetings with the building committee, the capital fund-raising committee and the architect.

Mark was under the wheel; time-strained. He was barely able to get his shut-in visits done this particular quarter as a result of the exciting confluence of the church renovation project. But a thought kept nagging at his mind. Elizabeth Crane, one of his grand old homebound members had recently come home from the hospital after suffering a mild stroke. And Mark hadn't seen her yet. Guilt was starting to work its way to the surface of Mark's conscience.

Nagging him was the fact that Elizabeth had actually called, inviting Mark to come to her home for a cup of tea. "I should have gone to see her without being called," he thought as he considered the invitation with pricked conscience.

Elizabeth had said over the phone, "I do understand, pastor, if you cannot come. I know you are a busy man, but if you have time, how wonderful it would be to share a cup of tea with you."

Despite his guilt Mark invented all sorts of reasons not to go to see Elizabeth. He had important meetings to attend: the County Helpline Board was meeting that afternoon and he was a member of the board; there was also a vacation Bible school meeting late into the afternoon and a district church meeting in the evening in a nearby city. He had almost justified his not going to see Elizabeth when he heard a voice in his inner ear. "Mark, you really need to go and see Elizabeth!" And so grudgingly, he went.

A glimmer of hope flashed across Mark's mind as he suddenly realized that Elizabeth wasn't coming to the door. "Oh, her daughter must have come and gotten her for her regular medical cleck-up," Mark considered with great anticipation. But just as he was about to turn and go, he heard footsteps and an intermittent crutch on the foyer floor. Waiting for the door to be opened, Mark stood, rigid.

"Come on in! I am so glad you could come, pastor. I know how busy you are. Please sit down in that chair over there. That one is much more comfortable," Elizabeth was simply delighted.

While they casually chatted, Mark recalled all of the old stuff he had seen in the comfortable parlor of previous visits. The old side board, he noticed the stately china cabinet, the lovely buffet filled with glittering cut glass and crystal. "Memories," he thought, what a marvelous precious life Elizabeth has had. Everyone in the parish loved Elizabeth. She had raised four children, had been a school teacher and her husband, Henry, had died some 10 years ago.

But Elizabeth's real priorities were evident throughout this room. Pictures of children and grandchildren were in and on every nook and cranny one could find. And the prize treasures were not the beautiful Hummels that were proudly displayed on the piano and in the curio cabinet, but the pictures and presents that the kids had made. They were clearly evident everywhere Mark looked. Whether on the coffee table or atop the end tables or tucked into the book shelves, the "kid projects" were proudly displayed. "Oh, this is the little hot plate my little Stephanie made for me. And this picture of a cat my little Jimmy colored for me, isn't it great? And over there on the shelf are all things my Sunday school children made for me over the years!"

After a little while Elizabeth said, "Let's go over to the dining room table to have our tea." As the two of them walked into the dining room, Mark was a bit nonplussed. The table was set with linen table cloth and silver. Not stainless steel but the stuff that Elizabeth must have retrieved from the handsome walnut box in the bottom drawer of her buffet cupboard. Sitting down at the table Mark noticed the table was set with linen napkins, china cups and saucers and even crystal goblets.

Elizabeth poured the tea and asked Mark, "Pastor, how about a nice freshly baked cinnamon roll with butter and some of my strawberry preserves." All of a sudden Mark found himself to be very hungry.

"These are the best cinnamon rolls I've ever had, Elizabeth," Mark intoned. And while they ate and drank they talked of things past, things present and what the future held for both of them. Elizabeth was also extremely interested in all of the church activities. She missed not being able to participate in the life of the congregation as she had once been able to do. But she still kept current on all of the activities. She took part where she was able, she was coordinator of the phone prayer chain and she continued to be an extremely good giver to the ministry and mission of the church.

As their conversation progressed a veil of complete joy settled upon Mark as he listened to Elizabeth. She was so intensely interested in every aspect of the church's ministry; she was thoroughly positive and encouraging. Mark smiled when Elizabeth demanded specifics. "I don't want generalities, pastor. I want all of the particulars," she crooned. "I want to know why our missionary is not being supported like he should be and what I can do to help," she continued forthrightly.

Elizabeth spoke with honesty and candor about the limitations imposed on her by the stroke. She spoke of her life and death. "You know pastor, I feel so fortunate to be a part of a servant community. An old friend once told me, 'Elizabeth, if you practice dying enough during your lifetime, you will hardly notice the difference when the actual time comes.' I've tried to live that way, pastor. I'm not afraid to die. I know God is right now walking with me in the valley of the shadow of death. My faith is everything to me, pastor."

Mark got a big lump in his throat, "That's beautiful, Elizabeth." And as Mark took his leave from that faithful home that day he thought, "I came here for a cup of tea and instead I received a banquet. I ate the bread of life."

Ordinary Time 21
John 6:60-69

Gunda

In the movie, *Days of Thunder,* Cole Thunder (Tom Cruise) when asked by his girlfriend why he races 200 miles per hour NASCAR stock cars, haughtily answers, "I want to be able to control that which is out of control." Our text for today raises the question: Are we unable to control anything? "What gives life is God's Spirit; man's power is of no use at all."

A little while later in the film, while in the middle of a heated argument because Cole has just previously chased a taxi cab, recklessly and violently, around a hotel parking lot, his girlfriend points her index finger at his face and says, "Listen Cole, you better wake up out of your little dream land and learn what everybody else in the world knows, that people are not in control of anything, we are finally and ultimately powerless, and the quicker you learn that lesson, my weak minded immature friend, the better off you will be!"

"What gives life is God's Spirit; man's power is of no use at all."

Not too many months ago, an entire nation said to its insensitive and manipulative leaders, "We are sorry, but as far as we're concerned you are not our leaders anymore because you do not have our best interests at heart. You are only concerned about your political futures. We are going to elect our own leaders who are compassionate toward our welfare and our country's welfare. And if you don't like it, then lump it. If you don't like it, shoot us, because life under your regime is worse than death anyway." The East German leaders ultimately discovered that they were powerless when they did not have anyone to "lord over." And the end result was a new East Germany as well as new leadership.

Walter Wink writes, "Many innocent people may die while the (demonic) powers appear to gain in invincibility with every death, but that is only an illusion. Their very brutality and desperation is evidence that their legitimacy is fast eroding. Their appeal to force is itself an admission that they can no longer command voluntary consent. Whenever sufficient numbers of people withdraw their consent, the (evil) powers inevitably fall."[1]

"What gives life is God's Spirit; man's power is of no use at all."

A story: Dr. Pennell stepped out of the door of the hospital. He had seen a group of men coming down the hill with a stretcher. "Whom are you bringing?" he asked the men as they lowered the stretcher in front of him.

The men shrugged their shoulders. "We don't know. We found the man lying by the side of the road. He is seriously wounded. Do you have room for him, Sahib?" We want to leave him here and continue on our way." The doctor bent over the man on the stretcher. He could tell that the patient was an Afghan, a member of the Patau tribe which was always at war with the surrounding population.

"Bring him in," said the doctor. "For him we have a bed." After the patient was settled, Dr. Pennell came to examine him.

"Sahib," moaned the patient, trying to tear the bandage off his eyes, "give me back my sight! Then I can go and find the man that did this to me. I want revenge! I want to kill him. After that I don't care whether I am blind the rest of my life! I just want revenge! Revenge! My enemy took my eyes. He will have to pay for it with his life. There is nothing more powerful than revenge!"

The doctor sat down beside his bed and told the man a story.

"Many years ago," he said, "the British government sent Captain Conolly as an envoy to Afghanistan. He never arrived in the capitol, however. On a lonely stretch of the road, he was seized by a tribe of that country. They took away his baggage, bound him, accused him of espionage, and threw him into prison. He had no idea what would happen to him.

"Weeks and months went by in terrible monotony. The guards mistreated him. The food was bad and very scarce. The only light he had in his cell came from a hole near the ceiling.

"In his misery he had only one comfort. That was a little prayer book that the guards had allowed Captain Conolly to keep. He had received it as a farewell gift from his sister when he left for India. The prayers and songs comforted him; he felt the presence of the Lord Jesus Christ in his cell.

"The prayer book did something else. Conolly was able to persuade the guards to give him a pen and something like ink to write with. Now he filled the margins of the little book with reports of his experience as a prisoner. He also wrote how he felt about those experiences and what effect they had on his soul. The prayer book became a diary of his prison life.

"A whole year passed by. The last entry in the prayer book was by someone else. It said that Conolly had been brought out of prison, publicly flogged, and then had been forced to dig his own grave.

"He was never seen again. No one except the tribe in Afghanistan knew about his execution. In vain his family and friends, and the government in England waited for some news of him. Twenty-one years went by.

"Then it so happened that one day a Russian officer was sauntering along a street in Buchara, a city in central Asia. He stopped in a second-hand shop. Among the odds and ends he discovered an English prayer book with all kinds of entries in the margins which he could not decipher. He saw a name and address on the flyleaf, however. 'Perhaps this little book is important to someone,' he thought to himself, and sent it to England.

"That is how Captain Conolly's sister received the prayer book which she had given to her brother 21 years before!

"With great anguish she read the account of the prison experience of her brother and was greatly moved by his thoughts during the days before his execution.

"What should she do? The terrible injustice done to her brother called for revenge. For Christian revenge! She was not wealthy, but she sent all the money that she could to Dr. Pennell's hospital with these instructions: 'Please keep a bed free in your hospital at all times for a sick or wounded Afghan, and use the money to take care of him until he regains his health. I am doing this in memory of my brother who suffered so much at the hands of Afghans and who died in their country.' "

There was complete silence at the bed of the wounded Afghan when Pennell had finished his story. The doctor put his hand on the shoulder of the blind man. "My friend," he said, "you are now lying in that bed. That you are being taken care of is a revenge for the death of Captain Conolly."

For the first time in his life, the man who so passionately desired revenge and who had so curtly rejected the message of Christ sensed a power that is stronger than hate. It is the power of love.[2]

"What gives life is God's Spirit; man's power is of no use at all."

A parable: Paul Dicerio sat nursing a glass of beer at Vero's Pub, a neighborhood bar with good food and a good reputation. In deep thought, he glanced over at the bulletin board near the entrance. The picture on the placard was of him. Paul was running for state senator and election day was tomorrow. "Vote Paul Dicerio for State Senator" the poster said in large bold capitals. "Boy, has it all been worth it?" Paul reminisced. He thought about the sacrifices he had made thus far. He had been away from his family every evening for the last six months; the meetings, the speeches, the time and the money. "Was it all worth it?" he continued to consider. "At every turn I've had to defend my reputation, respond to smear tactics," his thoughts rambled on. "To become a leader one somehow has to put one's self in compromising power positions," Paul's thoughts continued, "Money, power, prestige, a good old boy in the community ... is that what it really takes to get elected? What about integrity and decency and ethical values and compassion and common courtesy?" Paul's thoughts meandered almost out of control now. He felt tired. "I guess it's time to go home," he mused. But Paul Dicerio didn't get up from his bar stool. Because a name kept on nagging at his mind. Gunda Tobias. That name kept on flashing across his mind subliminally and uncontrollably.

"Now there is a powerful person," Paul thought to himself. "But certainly not the way I am powerful. She has very little money, she doesn't have a job title, she doesn't have any academic degrees, she is certainly not a good old boy and hardly prestigious," he thought. "What is it about Gunda Tobias?"

Gunda had grown up in poverty in Eastern Europe. She had come to the United States with nothing but immigration papers. Shortly after that she had married. Gunda and her husband William raised four children, and put them through college. Will had died 10 years ago leaving Gunda with more time than money to pursue her community volunteer efforts.

Paul's thoughts continued to gravitate and meditate on Gunda. "Now that woman has power," Paul thought to himself. He recalled two years ago when this small, stooped woman in a faded dress and well worn pumps was awarded the Citizenship Award for Outstanding Service in the County. The award was presented to Gunda in the glittering community banquet hall amidst the community's high rollers and influential people dressed in formal black and tasteful gowns. And the center of it all? A little old lady. Gunda Tobias. She was the one who received the Outstanding Service Award for her excellent work with bridge housing for the homeless over the past 15 years.

"No mayor or county commissioner or state representative holds the key to as much power as Gunda does in this community," Paul Dicerio murmured to himself. "She is rich. The most powerful weapon against the evils of this earth; the caring heart. The wealth of the compassionate spirit," Paul thought.

And then there was last year at the church council meeting the night Pastor Nelson suggested opening a day-care center in the church. Pastor Nelson went over his reasons: It was a good use of the building, it would attract young families, it was another source of income, and the Baptists down the street already had a day-care center. But Gunda stood up at the council meeting room table and changed the agenda from one of self-interest to one of moral and ethical integrity.

Gunda butted in, "Why is the church in the day-care business? How would this be a part of the ministry of the church?"

"Well, Gunda," said Neal Olson, "you know that it's getting harder every day to put food on the table. Both husband and wife must have full-time jobs."

"That's not true," said Gunda. "You know it's not true. It is not hard for anyone in this church, for anyone in this neighborhood, to put food on the table. There are people in this town for whom putting food on the table is quite a challenge, but I haven't heard any talk about them. If we are talking about ministry to them, then I'm in favor of the idea. No, what we're talking about is ministry to those for whom it has become harder every day to have two cars, a VCR, a place at the lake or a motor home. I just hate to see the church telling these young couples that somehow their marriage will be better or their family life more fulfilling if they can only get more stuff. The church ought to be courageous enough to say, 'That's a lie. Things don't make a marriage or a family.' "

"I wrestle with her impotence," Paul's mind continued, "but she just goes on changing the church, the community ... while I wish for more power and resources, she uses her power and resources to do what she can do at the moment ... 'what gives life is God's Spirit; man's power is of no use at all.' I think Saint John said that," Paul Dicerio reflected as he finally walked out of Vero's Pub. It was getting late. He had to get up early and go to the polls.[3]

[1] Walter Wink, "Waging Spiritual Warfare With the Powers," *Weavings,* Volume V, Number 2, March/April (1990), pp. 39-41.

[2] Adapted from *Staerker als Hass* in Hoeher als alle Vernunft by Anni Dyck (Basel: Agape-Verlag, 1965). Her source was Sammlung de Lange: Lillian Cox, "God's Mighty Men."

[3] Two sources inspired me in writing this parable. Some of the thoughts and monologue also came from the following sources: Robert Fulghum's essay on Mother Teresa in his book, *All I Really Need to Know I Learned in Kindergarten* and Stanley Hauerwas' and William H. Willimon's article in *The Christian Century*, titled "Ministry As More Than A Helping Profession," March 15, 1989.

Ordinary Time 22
Mark 7:1-8, 14-15, 21-23

Changing
The Rules

When I was a camp director the rules of long established and understood games were constantly being changed in order to incorporate a larger sphere of players. For the same reason Jesus said, "You have a clever way of rejecting God's law in order to uphold your own teaching." Jesus had a knack for constantly changing the rules of the game of life in order to incorporate a larger sphere of people in his kingdom net.

One such game where the rules were often changed was volleyball. Volleyball is a well-established game with rules which are basically understood by everyone who plays. Many times we would have children playing the game who were either handicapped or mentally retarded. In order to integrate these special children into the game of volleyball it was necessary to change the standing rules or laws of the game. We would say that it was fair for the special children to catch and throw the ball instead of having to volley the ball. This enabled all of the children to be part of the game.

In our text Jesus is concerned that all of his children are a part of his kingdom life. And he would go so far as to change the rules and regulations and laws in order to integrate as many of his children as possible. The Pharisees and teachers used the law to exclude people from the kingdom. This angered Jesus to the point of remembering what Isaiah had written: "These people honor me with their words, but their heart is really far away from me. It is no use for them to worship me, because they teach man-made rules as though they were my laws!''

Again, Jesus making a statement about how calcified and stiff the tradition had become. Jesus is saying here that because of love, his father would do anything to get his children into his spiritual kingdom net. God will even change the rules and regulations in order to include as many of his children as possible. Jesus says that the ancestors' love is bounded; that is, the tradition has become bounded by fear and selfishness, while God's love is unbounded and limitless. It is so much so that God even changes the law from being written on stone to being written on the heart.

I once read a story about a group of soldiers in France during World War II who had become separated from their platoon during a fierce battle to retake a village. The village was finally retaken but in the process one of their fellow soldiers was killed. The small motley group of men carried their dead comrade to the nearby village church. They sought out the pastor in order to ask him if he would grant permission to allow their friend to be buried in the church cemetery. The pastor asked the others if they knew if their dead friend had been baptized. They said that they did not know. The others explained to the pastor that they had talked a lot about life and death and God, but one subject they had not broached was if and when their comrade was baptized. "Well then," explained the pastor, "if you do not know if your friend was baptized I must inform you that church ecclesiology does not permit you to bury your dead friend in this cemetery."

Saddened by this news, the men carried the body to the edge of the cemetery and buried it on the other side of the fence.

The next morning the small rag-tag army walked over to the church cemetery to check the grave of their friend to make sure it hadn't been disturbed. They were all startled and disturbed when, after looking for quite some time, they could not find the fresh grave. Just as they were about to give up in utter frustration the pastor approached them and said, "You cannot find the grave because it is not there where you are looking for it. Yesterday, I felt really guilty after telling you that you could not bury your friend here in the cemetery. So I woke up very early this morning and moved the fence so that your comrade is now included in the church cemetery."

And Jesus said, "You put aside God's command and obey the teachings of men."

Jesus is making a startling and definitive point here. He is saying that his Father's love always preempts ancestral laws; that his new law of love written on the heart always preempts ancestral words written on stone.

Jesus is not saying that ritual cleanliness is bad or wrong in and of itself. We certainly practice, in our culture, similar sanitary measures. The point Jesus desires to make here is: what is unfriendly to God is when ritual cleanliness preempts God's love and mercy and compassion.

Jesus would have to put forbearance before forebears. He would have us participate in his father's love induced restraint ahead of ancestral legal tradition.

A story: The court warden's deep voice perked through to Billy's conscious awareness as he called the session of juvenile court to order. Billy had already sat through the arraignment session where he had been charged with aiding and abetting automobile vandalism. He felt really bad about the whole thing now. "But it's a bit late for that now," he thought to himself as he relived the incident that took place on New Castle Street two weeks ago.

"Jimmy and I were just out to have a good time cruising the neighborhood on foot that night. And then Jimmy just happens to bring his 22-caliber pistol with him. I didn't think anything of it at first. I mean, I didn't think he would actually take it out of the holster and start taking pot shots at stop signs and street lights. I just stood there with my stupid mouth swung wide open in disbelief. I couldn't believe what Jimmy was doing and I should have taken off home then running full speed ahead. But like a dummy I just stood there and gawked dumbfounded! And let him go on shooting at car tires and then he started to knock out windshields. You've gotta hand it to him. Jimmy is nuts! That's when the police showed up and put the handcuffs on both of us. And now here I am sitting in a juvenile court of law up on at least a dozen counts of vandalism."

Billy was nervous but never the less he was glad his mother was with him. That's what he felt most bad about. Disappointing his mother like this. She had worked extremely hard raising Billy and his sister and he couldn't bear to break her heart like this.

Through the clutter of ponderous guilt-ridden fog Billy heard his name, "Well, Billy," the judge said, "after reviewing your case do you have anything else you would like to say?"

With downcast eyes Billy shook his head in the negative and whispered softly, "I just feel so bad that I hurt my mother like this . . . and I know right from wrong . . . I shouldn't have let Jimmy do what he did . . . oh, I don't know Judge Green."

"Well, Billy," Judge Green said, "You're going to have to give me a few minutes in my office while I consider your case and what I think your sentence should be. I'll be back in 15 minutes. You can just wait right here, I won't be long."

The 15 minutes seemed like a lifetime to Billy, forcing him to deal with his crime once again. "Boy, I wish I could replay the tape on this one, but I guess I can't. I'll just have to take the medicine and live and learn. I'm never, ever going to get involved in anything like this again."

The sound of a door slamming against a door jamb snapped Billy back into the courtroom once again. Judge Green's formal black robe made him look official and authoritarian. And Billy didn't think he was going to like the medicine that was going to be dished out to him.

"Okay, Billy," Judge Green spoke intentionally, "here's what we're going to do. At least a dozen counts of automobile vandalism. I could send you to reform school for up to two years. You realize that don't you, Billy? You aided and abetted Jimmy, you know?"

Judge Green continued, "But I'm not going to do that, Billy. Do you want to know why?" Billy vaguely nodded his head in the affirmative. "Let me tell you why, Billy," Judge Green was speaking softly and tenderly now, "I've known your mother for a long time. Yes, your mother and I went to school together when we were kids. Billy, your father was a fine man, but when he suddenly died 10 years ago that left all of the responsibility on your mother. Billy, your mother has done a fine job raising you and your sister."

Billy reached over and grabbed his mother's hand and held it gently. The judge continued, "She's done an excellent job despite the handicap of not having your father during all these years. Billy, she has sacrificed for you. She has worked hard, overtime, in order to give you the things that you need to have. And she has raised you in the church and made sure that you were active in positive organizations like the scouts and school athletics and school clubs. And most importantly, Billy, she has spent good time with both you and your sister. She's always made it a priority to take the two of you on a vacation every summer. Billy, your mother has done a darn good job with you! And I'm going to show restraint in this case. Not, mind you, because of you. What you did, Billy, is unconscionable. I am not going to send you to reform school, Billy. But I am sentencing you to 60 hours of voluntary community service in the city's park and recreation department's summer program. Case dismissed!"

"You put aside God's command and obey the teachings of men."

Likewise, God displays his forbearance and shows his restraint. Not because of us or what we have done or not done. But because of Christ and what he has done for us through his life, death and resurrection.

God's love, shown to us in Jesus, preempts rules, regulations and ancestral laws. God's new law written on stone. Thus today we do not celebrate your ancestral forebears but instead we celebrate God's gracious display of friendship toward humanity through his active forbearance, through his restraint.

Ordinary Time 23
Mark 7:31-37

The Spiritual Organ Of Corti

Jonah went in the opposite direction of that in which God wanted him to go. Jonah was jealous of God's unbounded desire to include even the evil city of Nineveh in his kingdom. Like the older brother in Jesus' parable of the prodigal son, Jonah wouldn't hear or speak of God's gracious redemptive sweep, which included even prodigals and foreigners. So, through a great fish, God opened up Jonah's ears so that he would be able to speak God's word of repentance and redemption.

"He even causes the deaf to hear and the dumb to speak!"

Likewise, Saul, on his way to Damascus to single out Christians for persecution, met God face to face. Blind and deaf to God's gracious and redemptive power, the Lord came crashing into his life on that road. His entire world was flipped upside down. Jesus touched Paul's tongue so that he could tell, without any trouble, the entire world about God's amazing grace.

A friend who lives in an area of the country where there are many Native American Indian reservations, attended a church conference years ago. One of the workshops that he attended at the conference concerned the plight of the Native American Indian population as a minority group and how they have been completely forgotten. My friend decided to attend this particular workshop because he happened to live in an area where there were many reservations. His attitude at the time was that he simply wanted to learn more about the issue. He did not necessarily desire to do anything about the problem. Then, right smack in the middle of the seminar, a well-known member of the American Indian Movement entered the room where they were gathered and threw a brick in the center of the meeting table. The crashing monolith startled the assembly. The man from AIM said to the people that all they did was talk and study, study and talk, but they never really did a darn thing about the prevailing issues. My friend was certainly not impressed by this man's overt action. In fact, my friend was a bit offended. But when he returned home he couldn't get the incident out of his mind. He kept on asking himself, "Well, what can I do about it? I'm only one person." Gradually his ears were opened and one day he decided to speak. In fear and trepidation, my friend boldly drove his car north to one of the nearby reservations to visit with a local chief. And that was just the beginning of a 25-year ministry to Native American Indians in the area of the country in which he lives. My friend has been very instrumental and active in the planning and implementation of WIRC (Wisconsin Indian Resource Council). He has also been involved in Operation Black Dirt, a corporation established to incubate Native American Indian-owned small businesses. Today, my friend tells me that Christ caused his deaf ears to hear and then gave him the courage to speak on behalf of the American Indian population. It has not been easy for my friend. As you can well imagine, his inclusive actions have caused him to be ostracized from former friends and associates. But he tells me that it has been worth it because, as he puts it, "I was dumb but now I can speak God's truth."

A story: Telemachus was a monk who lived in Asia Minor about the year AD 400. During his life the gladiatorial games were very popular. The gladiators were usually slaves or political prisoners who were condemned to fight each other unto death for the amusement of the crowd. People were fascinated by the sight of spurting blood.

Telemachus was very much disturbed that the Christian Emperor Honorius sponsored these games and that so many people who called themselves Christians went to see them. What could be further from the Spirit of Christ than the horrible cruelty of the gladiatorial games? The church was opposed to the games and spoke out against them, but most people would not listen because they were deaf to God's unbounded message of love.

Telemachus realized that talking about this evil was not enough. It was time to do something. But what could he accomplish — one lone monk against the whole Roman Empire? He was unknown. He had no power. And the games had been entrenched in Roman life for centuries. Nothing that he could possibly do would ever make a difference.

For a long time Telemachus agonized about the problem. Finally he could not live with himself any longer. For the integrity of his own soul he decided to obey Christ's Spirit within him, regardless of the consequences. He set out for Rome.

When Telemachus entered the city, the people he met had gone mad with excitement. "To the Coliseum! The games are about to begin!"

Telemachus followed the crowd. Soon he was seated among all the other people. Far away in a special place he saw the emperor.

The gladiators came out into the center of the arena. Everybody was tense. Everybody was quiet. Now the two strong young men drew their swords. The fight was on! One of them would probably die in a few minutes. Who would it be?

But just at that moment, Telemachus rose from his seat and ran into the arena. He held high the cross of Christ and threw himself between the two combatants.

"In the name of our Master," he cried, "Stop fighting!" The two men hesitated. Nothing like this had ever happened before. They did not quite know what to do.

But the spectators were furious. Telemachus had robbed them of their anticipated entertainment! They yelled wildly and stampeded toward the center of the arena. They became a mob. With sticks and stones they beat Telemachus to death.

Far down there in the arena lay the little battered body of the monk. Suddenly the mob grew quiet. A feeling of revulsion at what they had done swept over them. Their once deaf ears sensed a stirring. Emperor Honorius rose and left the coliseum. The people followed him. Abruptly the games were over.

Honorius sensed the mood of the crowd. His ears too were opened. He issued an edict forbidding all future gladiatorial games. Honorius' ears had been opened to the violence and dehumanization of the games. As a result he was able to speak.

So it was that in about the year A.D. 404, because one individual, filled with the love of Christ, dared to say no, all gladiatorial games ceased.[1]

To hear one must have an effective organ of corti inside one's ear. A defective corti will not produce sound that is audible.

Likewise, one must have an effective "spiritual corti" if one is to spiritually hear. A defective spiritual corti will not produce sound that is spiritually audible.

Jesus is saying that he is our spiritual organ of corti which allows us to hear spiritually. Jesus touches our ears and tongue so that we can spiritually hear and speak his Word.

A friend of mine often tells me that he is not very proud of his younger adult life. Regarding those days he says that he was belligerent, hot tempered, quick to judge others, arrogant, vulgar, obnoxious, and more than once spent a night in jail for fighting.

Then one day he was involved in a serious automobile accident. He was seriously injured. Suffering severe swelling of the brain he underwent emergency neurosurgery to relieve the pressure pushing against the cranium. The surgery was somewhat successful but he experienced acute memory loss as a result of the brain operation.

My friend put it this way, "I had lost my memory but I wasn't so far gone that I didn't know I had lost it. So for the first time in my life I got down on my knees and asked God to give me back my mind. And if God gave me back my mind I promised I would join a church and worship and serve him."

Allow me to digress: Isn't it interesting that very often we get what we ask for when we pray? Sometimes we end up not liking what we asked for to begin with. If we pray and ask for a meaningful ministry, God just may answer that prayer by dumping us into a mission field where we do not desire to be. But that's exactly what he had asked for to begin with; a meaningful and challenging ministry. My friend got exactly what he asked for. Yes, he had lots of faults, but he was a man of his word. He was a man of integrity. So he was challenged, by God, to keep his promise, not for salvation's sake but in response to God's gracious gift of physical life.

That was 20 years ago. My friend is still active in the same church where he became a member in response to God's intervention in his recovery. He continues, to this day, to serve gladly and diligently. He tells me that the Lord God gave him back his hearing. Now he can go and tell others about Christ, the spiritual organ of corti, who enables all who are open, discernment of the kingdom.

"At once the man was able to hear, his speech impediment was removed, and he began to talk without any trouble."

---

[1] Adapted from *Peace Be With You* by Cornelia Lehn, Faith and Life Press, Newton, Kansas, "What Can One Person Accomplish?" p. 27. Previously adapted from a story in *Courage In Both Hands* by Allen A. Hunter (Fellowship of Reconciliation, 21 Audubon Ave., New York 32, N.Y.)

Ordinary Time 24
Mark 8:27-35

God's Math: Lose Life = Save It

When self-preservation is our central aim, we are never safe. However, when we are committed to surrender to the disturbances that Godly compassion produces we are never in danger.

So Jesus said, "For whoever wants to save his own life will lose it; but whoever loses his life for me and for the gospel will save it."

We can be dumped into the most precarious situations but if God is with us we are not in danger. The worst that can happen to us is dislocation from Christ.

Hence, as long as we are with the eternal divine logos, the infinite "Word become flesh" in the Lord Jesus, our thoughts come from God, not from man.

But as we see in the lesson, this eternal relationship with the "Word become flesh" is easily tarnished.

"Jesus rebuked Peter, 'Get away from me Satan,' he said, 'Your thoughts don't come from God but from men!' "

Peter did not yet have the spiritual perception to see that the by-product of Jesus' suffering and death would be resurrection power and growth.

And so Jesus uses this experience as an opportunity to teach the disciples a lesson. Notice how Jesus took Peter aside but looked at the other disciples while he rebuked Peter. This was a pedagogical moment for Jesus. An opportunity to both give the disciples an idea of suffering servanthood and to challenge them to discern a deeper spiritual perspective. That life is in giving, not getting.

Even after his confession, "You are the Messiah," Peter continued to live in the human world of illusion. He could not yet see beyond his shadow.

There is a fable about a man who lived in the desert. He would wake up every morning and follow his shadow. So as the sun moved across the sky from east to west the man essentially walked in a large oval. At sundown he ended up where he had started. This continued for years. The man walked in circles day after day, following his shadow. One night the man heard the voice of God in a dream while he slept. The voice told him to stop following his shadow. Instead, "Follow the sun," the voice challenged, "And you will experience life as you have never dreamed it could be."

The man thought for many days about his vision of God while he continued to walk around in circles in the desert. But one day he mustered up enough courage to break away from his shadow. Little by little, step by step, the man began to follow the sun. And he discovered a kingdom that was, heretofore, way beyond his wildest dreams and imagination. Ultimately, he became friends with the Son.

"For whoever wants to save his own life will lose it; but whoever loses his life for me and the gospel will save it."

Alfred Delp says it this way, just prior to his execution by the Nazis for his participation in the "Kreisau Circle," a moderate resistance group dedicated to the reconstruction of Germany along Christian lines after the war: "Up to now the Lord has helped me wonderfully. I am not yet scared and not yet beaten. The hour of human weakness will no doubt come and sometimes I am depressed when I think of all the things I hoped to do. But I am now a man internally free and far more genuine and realized than I was before. Only now have I sufficient insight to see the thing as a whole."[1]

Thus Jesus proposes his mathematics, his economics: Save life = lose life; Lose life = save it.

A friend related this story to me. My friend's mother-in-law helped him understand this equation. My friend married an only child. On their wedding day his mother-in-law told him: "I have been so blessed by God! If I were to die today I would have received the greatest gifts that anyone could have received: a gracious and loving family and caring friends and a God who has redeemed me."

The irony of this (not so ironic when you consider it from God's perspective: lose life = save life) is that she was the one who was always giving. She was the one who was always losing her life. She was the one who was always dying for the sake of others. And hence she was the one who was joy-filled!

Today, the mother-in-law lives at an Alzheimer's center. She cannot remember what she ate for lunch five minutes ago nor can she remember what day it is. But there is a twinkle in her eyes. A twinkle that tells of God's economy. Namely, lose life = save it.

The twinkle says it loud and clear. Happiness and joy come with losing one's life in service. And that is real power. Power that transforms resides in the generous and compassionate person. The person who practices dying, for others, during their lifetime.

A tribute: Such a normal, almost banal day. Justin thought as he sluggishly climbed into the family's white Trans Am to go to work. He worked on the grounds crew at a golf course. A summer job, between semesters at the university, which he kind of liked except for the early 5 a.m. time he was required to pull out of his driveway in order to make it to work on time. He wouldn't be doing this for very long anyway, he thought, as he considered that in only six weeks he would be back in school. The day's date was June 29 and on August 18 he would be sitting in his dorm room counting the many books he would be required to read the following fall semester. He had great expectations of being an engineer just like his father.

Suddenly and startlingly Justin's musings and broodings were cut short by an oncoming vehicle rounding a sharp curve in the road and crossing over into his lane. The pickup truck was coming toward him head on. Justin needed a place to go so he quickly swerved onto the shoulder of the road. The Trans Am hit a jagged edge of the berm, blowing a tire. The car flipped over, end over end. The last thing Justin remembered was being upside down before he blacked out.

A passer-by saw what happened and immediately summoned a state trooper and an ambulance on his radio. Recognizing Justin, the eyewitness also went to a neighbor and called his father. Jim, Justin's father, was at the scene in a matter of minutes, arriving shortly after the trooper. The officer briskly walked over to Jim's car, "You must be the boy's father. I'm Trooper A. A. Michael. The paramedics are working on your son, but I'm sorry, I think it's too late. He was gone when we arrived on the scene." Tears welled up in Jim's eyes. Trooper Michael continued, "But I'm here to ask you for a favor, Jim. As I told you before, my name is A.A. Michael, that is, Arch Angel Michael and I'm stationed at the barracks in the kingdom."

Haltingly, Jim stammered, "Please continue." Sobbing, he said, "You said something about wanting a favor."

Trooper Michael said, "Yes, I did. But it's more like a trade. I have orders to ask you to trade your life here on earth for your son's life."

Jim looked bewildered. "What do you mean, trade my life for his?"

Michael continued, "I mean that Gabriel, our football coach was asked to be Saint Peter's full time coach. Pete never could play golf very well. We are in desperate need of a good football coach. The Lord wants you, Jim. Only you! He told me to get you whatever it takes, so here I am."

Jim looked at Trooper Michael as if he were nuttier than a fruit cake. Jim was stunned. "What kind of setup was this?" he thought.

Trooper Michael continued, "I told the Lord that we would never be able to get you because of your important commitments in your church, community, family and school, especially your football coaching responsibilities. But the Lord grew quite impatient because he wanted only you, just you. He says you're the only man with the right stuff — you know — the right kind of integrity to be our new head football coach. The Lord reminded me that the team has never lost a national championship and he does not intend to start losing to the dark forces of the universe now. So when this happened," Trooper Michael pointed to the overturned car, "I came right away because I thought you would agree to a trade. Justin gets to finish living out his life here on earth, you get to be head coach of the greatest football team in the cosmos, the Lord gets the head coach he desires and everybody is happy, everyone wins!"

Jim was bewildered by all of this, but he knew he didn't have a choice. He wanted, in the worst way, for Justin to experience the same fulfilling life on earth that he had had. "You said nobody loses, but what about my wife, Karen, and my other children?"

Trooper Michael spoke softly and tenderly now, "Your engineering business is in good hands with your two oldest sons. Yes, I agree that it is not quite fair for Karen and your one daughter who still lives at home, but remember they will not sorrow too long. Oh yes, they will sorrow for a little while because they will miss you. But let me remind you that you will all be reunited again in the future.

Then without hesitation, Jim said, "When do you want me?"

Michael considered this for a moment and then said, "Summer football camp starts the first of August, but we can give you a few extra days to get your affairs in order. How does August fifth sound to you? That way you can be at camp on Monday, the sixth."

"Okay," Jim said.

An exhilarating yell came from one of the paramedics, "He's going to make it! I don't believe it. A miracle! He's going to make it! I can't believe we resuscitated him."

Jim never really finalized things. The last 36 days of his life were loved like all the rest. He didn't need to change the way in which he lived and gave to his family. He didn't have to change the way in which he served his community. He didn't need to change the way in which he was committed to the church. He didn't have to change the way he coached football and was a friend, and for some a father, to the players. He didn't have to change the way he ran his business. He didn't have to change the way in which everyone he related with he made feel special and loved because of the interest and concern he showed. He didn't need to change the way in which he gave of himself; the way in which he daily lost his life in service to others.

Jim didn't do anything different. So he didn't tell anyone. He just lived his life the way he had always lived it — with integrity — and on August 5, he was simply enveloped by the Lord's Spirit. He had a heart attack and died instantly. Jim is now serving the Lord as a coach for the greatest team in all of history. The team's legacy is even more spectacular than the Green Bay Packers and the Pittsburgh Steelers.

On August 7 hundreds of people came to pay their respects to this very gracious man and coach. On August 8, the Lord held a going away party for Jim at his church; Emmanuel Church, God with us! And what a party it was![2]

---

[1] Alfred Delp, "After The Verdict," *Weavings,* Volume IV, Number 3, May/June (1989), 28-29.

[2] This story is told in the memory of Jim Trettle, a friend and one who knew God's mathematics: Lose life = save it. Jim's son Justin, was in fact, pulled from a near fatal automobile accident just weeks before his father's death.

Ordinary Time 25
Mark 9:30-37

A Formula For Greatness

Following the creation of man and woman, it is not surprising in Genesis 1:28 to find guidelines as to how we are to use our time in the caring of creation. We are reminded that our Judeo-Christian tradition and heritage participate in and include time. We are reminded that salvation is bound to a continuous time process which embraces the past, the present and the future, as well as people and earth (land). Looking at Genesis 1:28, we see the word multiply. In Hebrew it is *yabah* and it does not mean to multiply our earth with so many people that we overwhelm our environment. Instead, the Hebrew word *yabah* means "to grow in wisdom and sensitivity." The Hebrew word for fill is *mahleh*, and it does not mean to fill the air with pollution. *Mahleh* means "to bring a gift to the earth." *Cabash* is the Hebrew word for subdue and it does not mean to deplete the soil by over-use or erosion or to kill animals indiscriminately or to manipulate and dehumanize individuals. *Cabash* means "to put weight on, to rub tenderly as you would when you knead bread or when you give one you love a back rub." *Radah* was the Hebrew word for "irrigation person." Literally, it means to "make function properly." The irrigation person was the one who controlled the locks on the irrigation dam. This was a very important job because this person made the precious irrigation water "function" and "flow" properly. A better translation of Genesis 1:28 might be: "Be fruitful and mature, grow in wisdom and sensitivity, bring a gift to the earth, rub the earth tenderly, and make it function properly so that the fish in the sea and the birds in the air, and the animals, and the forests, and the lakes, and the rivers, and the streams, and all people will continue to become good!"

Hence, God's first words spoken to humanity was the formula for greatness. God desires us to see our work, mission and ministry as stewardship and care-taking; taking care of creation and accepting this responsibility as persons created in the image of God. This means understanding our community, our activity, our economics, our managing the household, our work as a gift of responsibility given to us by God.

"Who is the greatest?" Those who are responsible stewards of God. "Who is the greatest?"

"Whoever wants to be first must place himself last of all and be the servant of all."

Jesus points out that greatness is an elusive gift. This is because when we think we are great we are not, but the reciprocal of this axiom does provide for the gift of greatness: when we do not think we are great we are then open and free to be great.

"And Jesus humbled himself and became obedient even unto death, even death on a cross. Therefore God has highly exalted him ..."

The fact that the disciples were arguing among themselves as to who was the greatest implicates them: they are not great. Jesus implies that if they were truly great they would not be arguing about greatness.

Jesus said to them, "Whoever wants to be first must place himself last of all and be servant of all."

Thus greatness in the kingdom is always completely unselfconscious. That is to say that when we are about what we should be doing as disciples, being compassionate stewards and servants, we touch other's lives with a kind of kingdom greatness that we are totally aware of.

You have all received a letter like the one I am going to share. I received a letter from a former camp counselor who worked as a part of my camp staff for several summers. The letter came "out of the blue!" I had not heard from John for several years. And then this letter from him appeared in my mail box. John told me, in the letter, what a positive influence my ministry to him was. It was because of me he had sought a Christian vocation and was soon to graduate from seminary. He wrote to say thank you and to tell me that I was great. I was just doing my job. The job that God spells out in Genesis 1:28. Greatness is always unselfconscious in the kingdom of God.

A story: Victor reminisced as he sat in his eclectic Victorian office in the old ivy hollowed administration building on the university campus.

Today was Victor's 65th birthday. His retirement would be official at 5 p.m. that afternoon. His thoughts meandered and lingered over the past 43 years. For 15 years he was a public school teacher. At first he taught in a one-room school house: first through eighth grade. Then as school consolidations took place he taught fifth grade.

He then applied for and received a fellowship to attend graduate school. The next three years were spent studying at the University of Nebraska. After much hard work and burning the midnight oil the dissertation was finally approved by his doctoral committee.

Following graduate school, Victor was offered the position of registrar at the university. So Victor and his wife, Marion, and his two children, Susan and Gary, moved to Statesville.

Victor had been the registrar at the university for 25 years. They had been good years. Yes, pain-filled at times, especially switching the entire registration process from manual to an automated computer system, but good! "I would do it all over again," he thought.

Victor had worked and counseled with literally thousands of students during his 25-year tenure. He had helped students formulate their schedules and curriculum and major tracks. Conscientiously, Victor met each year with every freshman and junior to make sure they were meeting all the necessary requirements for graduation by the end of their senior year.

Higher education was expensive and Victor wanted to make sure that each of his students was progressing through his or her schedules as efficiently as possible, while at the same time, meeting all of their goals and expectations while at the university.

Yes, at times it all had been very difficult, always time consuming. He took a personal interest in each student. And that could be extremely fatiguing at times. But Victor was a dedicated university administrator and loved the challenge of actively taking part in shaping young adult minds and lives.

Just the other day a colleague asked him, "Well, Victor, you're hanging it up next week for good. Would you do it all again?"

Victor's response had been, "Sure, I would do it again!"

His wanderings interrupted by a knock on his office door, Victor said, "Come on in!"

"There's someone here to see you Dr. Pagenkopf," said his secretary. An expression of quiet surprise was scarcely visible on her face. It's one of your former students, Scott Bond. You remember Scotty, don't you?" Sarah asked, tactfully attempting to jar Victor's memory.

Victor looked at Scotty for a split second, hastily putting his mind in gear and placing him in a proper context and approximate year he would have graduated. The university graduated a couple thousand students every year.

A light suddenly flickered on in Victor's mind, "Oh Scotty, it's great to see you! Yes, I remember we worked very hard getting your school schedule to fit with your work study program. But we finally were able to coordinate everything and you graduated on schedule. Well, tell me about yourself. Where do you live? What are you doing now? You married? Do you have a family?" Victor chuckled, "I'm doing all the talking and won't even give you a chance to answer."

"Well, Dr. Pagenkopf, I am married and have two beautiful daughters. They're sweethearts, you know, daddy's little girls. I am the county human services director now, in Lake City. I love my job and Lake City is a great place to raise children."

Victor had a great big smile on his face, "Oh Scotty, that's great, I'm so happy for you!"

"Dr. Pagenkopf," Scotty continued soberly, "I didn't necessarily stop to see you today to tell you what I am doing professionally. Oh, I did want to tell you that too, but I really came to see you today because I read in the alumni newsletter that today is your last day. And I just wanted to tell you that I would not have graduated if it hadn't been for you. There's so much to say and so very little time that I wanted to make sure I told you what I'm about to say before you officially retire.

"Remember when I was a student here I told you my father was a steel worker all of his life? In fact, he was the first black person to be promoted to supervisor in his department. He worked darn hard to put me and my brother and two sisters through college. But there was never quite enough money so we all had to be on work study programs in order to make it through school. For a while I thought I was going to have to drop out my junior year because my classes and my job didn't integrate together. Remember I came to you for help? And you took such a personal interest in my predicament. You helped me work things out and I finally graduated with honors. Dr. Pagenkopf, I came here today to say thank you! You are a great person!" Scotty was a bit choked up, "You saved my life."

Victor was nonplussed and taken back by Scotty's kind and compassionate words. In fact, Victor was speechless. He didn't know what to say. The only thing he could do for the first 30 seconds was get teary eyed. It was an overwhelming joy filled cry. "I was just doing my job, Scotty. Every student in this university deserves dignity and understanding and a listening ear. That's all I did, give each and every one of my students what they earned and deserved. They respected me, and I respected them back."

Tears clearing away, Victor thoughtfully looked at Scotty and said, "Thank you, Scotty! You are too kind. That's the best gift I could ever receive on my last day of school."

Victor and Scotty said good-bye and embraced. As Scotty left Victor said to himself, "A fine young man, and to think that I helped him get through the university." Victor chuckled to himself and continued to pack boxes with books and papers and mementoes.

His thoughts continued to ramble, "It will be good to spend more time going to auctions, refinishing antiques and working at my painting and rosemaling."

A post script: That evening Marion, Victor's wife, had a surprise retirement party for Victor. He received one gift. Marion had sent letters to Victor's former students asking them to make a copy of their diploma and transfer it onto a piece of old white bed sheet or pillow case. During the months that she received the diploma squares she fashioned them into a wall hanging. The problem was that the wall hanging was so large that it couldn't be opened up entirely in their house where the party was. It contained thousands of diplomas of Victor's former students. So today the wall hanging is on display on a wall in the university field house. It would be an understatement to say that Victor was remarkably surprised.

The wall hanging reminds all who gaze upon it and understand, of the answer to the question, "Who is the greatest?"

"Whoever welcomes in my name one of these children, welcomes me; and whoever welcomes me, welcomes not only me but also the one who sent me."

Ordinary Time 26
Mark 8:38-43, 45, 47-48

When Is It Tolerable To Be Intolerant?

By Donald Macleod

Two words in our vocabulary conjure up opposite types of persons: the tolerant and the intolerant. One seems to wear a white hat; the other, a black one. Two little verses set these types in clear contrast. Jonathan Swift wrote:

We are God's chosen few.
All others will be damned;
There is no place in heaven for you,
We can't have heaven crammed.

Edwin Markham wrote:

He drew a circle that shut me out —
Rebel, heretic, thing to flout.
But Love and I had the wit to win —
We drew a circle that took him in.

These two attitudes underlie this passage in Mark's gospel. Here we note three groups of sayings of Jesus, each of which suggests either the presence or absence of tolerance.

First of all (vv. 38-40), we have Jesus' disciple, John, coming to him and raising a complaint. John and his brother, James, were sons of Zebedee and were nicknamed "Sons of Thunder," because they were somewhat precipitous in their actions and judgments. What upset John this time was the sight of a man, who was not a member of the disciples' group, exorcising a demon from another man and doing so in the name of Jesus. The belief current at that time was that "if one could get to know the name of a still more powerful spirit, and then command the evil demon in that name to come out of a person, the demon was supposed to be powerless to resist." (William Barclay) Jesus' response to John was a cryptic remark: "He that is not against us is for us." That settled the case of John's intolerance.

And so with us. Intolerance stalks our footsteps whenever, in life's affairs, we condemn people who do not do everything our way. For example, take our Christian worship in all its multiple forms and practices. Don't we still have, in our churches, people who say to their neighbor, "You worship God in your way, but I'll worship him in his"? Intolerance scowls and says there is only one way to God — mine! Others have no right do their own thinking. "It's a fearful thing," writes Dr. Barclay, "for any man or any church to think that he or it has a monopoly on salvation." And G. Johnstone Jeffrey commented, "See that you do not deny the name of Christian to another because he or she is not wearing your label, denominational, ecclesiastical or theological." Christian tolerance invites us to sit down together and assess our beliefs and doctrines by the kind of people they produce, by what these do for human need, and how limited really are our little ideas in the face of Christian truth. Bare intolerance has no place in Christian thinking for, as Dr. Barclay commented further, "Every man in need has a claim upon us because every man is dear to Christ."

Second (vv. 43-48), Jesus indicates the dangers that lie in tolerance, in *laissez-faire*, in indifference to things as they are regardless of their obvious insufficiency. Always Jesus set before his disciples the greatest goal of all, namely, life; and for him that meant being in the kingdom of God. What was meant by the kingdom? Simply this: wherever God's will was recognized and done. In his prayer given to the disciples, the petition reads, "Thy will be done on earth as it is in heaven." Now this is not attained by our own wisdom, talents or powers. It is received as a by-product of faith, commitment and complete surrender. But this does not mean we can remain inactive, nor is it suggested that we can tolerate allowing our spiritual capacities to continue in a half-developed state. Discipline, self-denial and sacrifice are meant to prevent any organ, spiritual or bodily, getting in the way of our goal. We are not to tolerate the do-nothingness of lazy tolerance. G. K. Chesterton reminded us, "Merely having an open mind is nothing." All of us must stand for something or else we shall fall for anything. Ours must be a discriminating tolerance.

Third (vv. 49, 50), Jesus talks metaphorically and uses, as his idiom, salt, an element very familiar to his people because of the role it played in their whole culture and economy. The idea here is that there needs to be an intolerance of tolerance. And the character and activity of salt illustrate aptly what Jesus meant. The Christian life is not all softness, relaxation and "me-too-ism." There must be salt in it, for salt, like fire, has a purifying function. Moreover, it brings out inherent flavor and preserves what might otherwise decay. For us, in daily life, G. J. Jeffrey wrote about salt, "There must be something in it comparable to the stinging saltness of the sea-breeze, smarting, stimulating, giving tone to our whole system."

Here is implied, moreover, that for you and me to be truly Christian we must have strong convictions about what we believe and about how we act and why. They must not be wishywashy and tolerant of all fuzzy opinions and attitudes. Jesus said, "Have salt in yourselves, and be at peace with one another." This is the happy combination of an informed intolerance and a balanced tolerance. An open mind is a tolerant one, but it cannot tolerate that which prevents it from becoming and continuing in what life in God's kingdom requires. "Sooner or later," wrote Ned Rorem, "you've heard all your best friends have to say. Then comes the tolerance of real love."

Donald Macleod is author of this homily. He is the former Francis L. Patton Professor of Preaching and Worship at Princeton Theological Seminary, Princeton, New Jersey. This homily was originally published in Know The Way, Keep The Truth, Win The Life, *(CSS 7858).*

Ordinary Time 27
Mark 10:2-16

Learning
The Basics

The Pharisees came up "to trap Jesus" and they asked him, "Is it lawful for a man to divorce his wife?" Jesus in response asked them what Moses had taught, and they replied correctly that Moses had said a man could simply give his wife a certificate of divorce and that was all there was to it. (Deuteronomy 24:1-4, was designed originally to protect the wife and guarantee her a certain amount of freedom.) Jesus was between a "rock and a hard place." If he answered "yes" to the question he would be promoting marital irresponsibility, and if he answered "no" to the question he would be disagreeing with Moses, the greatest patriarch of Israel.

However, Jesus would not permit the question to be turned into a contest between himself and Moses. So he set the question in the context of God's purpose. God's act should not be mollified by people's action, even if it is legal. We are all familiar with the "rule book syndrome." On the Little League field, adults attempt and get away with as much as possible by quoting and spouting the rule book "on in through the night." Marriage, Jesus said, had been established by God from the beginning of creation; and for this man was to leave father and mother and be joined to his wife. By the miracle of love, the two should become one. (Mark 10:6-8)

"What therefore God has joined together, let no one put asunder." (Mark 10:9)

Taking this thought one step further, Paul says that marriage is a matter of mutual respect!

The consideration of Ephesians 5:21-31 will sensitize us to the notion that Paul was not about to play into the hands of the Pharisaic trap of Mark 10. Ephesians 5 is part of what is called a "household code" during the time of Jesus. Typically these so-called "household codes" spelled out the rights and obligations of husbands and wives, parents and children, and masters and slaves. "Household codes" were very common kinds of writings in the Roman Empire of Jesus' time. Hence, there is nothing uniquely Christian about this practice or instruction that wives should be submissive to their husbands. Simply everyone in the Jewish or Greco-Roman world, of the time of Jesus, would have agreed and insisted upon it! The point is that we who express ourselves in different ways ought not to blame the writer of Ephesians for repeating what was a common and general assumption of his time and day.

To illustrate, allow me to turn the tables! Suppose I explained to Paul that, "after church I need to hurry up and go to work at the office." Paul would probably respond, "Work on the Sabbath! Unheard of! How uncivilized!" Just as people during Jesus' day would not understand why most of our stores and shops are open on our Sabbath, we in turn, in our time today, have a difficult time understanding how the writer of Ephesians could possibly say, "Wives must totally submit themselves to their husbands."

As a new "follower of the way," Paul has done something extremely new! He has taken the cultural assumption of his day, "so is a husband the head of his wife; and as the church submits to Christ, so should wives to their husbands, in everything," and given it a new twist.

We must continue on and read more. "Be subject to one another out of reverence for Christ." (5:21) "Husbands should love their wives just as Christ loved the church and sacrificed himself for her to make her holy." (5:25)

In a world where husbands by law and custom had absolute power over their wives these words were revolutionary! In Jesus' time, Hebrew culture held that wives were mere chattel, property that was owned. A wife could be given a writ of divorce for simply burning the dinner or not being pretty enough. Thus, the good news of the gospel intrudes upon the conventional proper posture of Jesus' day.

Recall Philemon who was a prominent Christian and owner of a slave named Onesimus. This slave had run away from his master, and then had come in contact with Paul, who was then in prison. Through Paul, Onesimus the slave became a Christian. Paul's letter to Philemon is an appeal to Philemon to be reconciled to his slave, whom Paul is sending back to him, and to welcome him not only as a forgiven slave but as a Christian brother. Paul refers to Philemon as "[your] brother in Christ," (Philemon 1:8) and then speaks of Onesimus, "who is my own son in Christ." (Philemon 1:10) Since Philemon is a brother to Paul and Onesimus is a son to Paul, Philemon doesn't have a choice but to take his slave back graciously with loving open arms. In other words, we can pick our friends but we can't choose our relatives as Christians. We have no other choice but to treat another with love and respect and integrity. This is why the writer of Ephesians boldly asserts, "Be subject to one another out of reverence for Christ," despite the norms and order of the day!

These words are not the usual words we are used to hearing when two people work at living their lives together in marriage. The market economy talks in terms of freedom, while the planned economy talks in terms of equality. The gospel writers, however, do not speak in terms of these categories of freedom and equality. They instead constantly speak in terms of relationships; mutual respect and love toward one another.

One text calls husbands and wives to defer to one another and love one another out of "reverence for Christ!" The Hebrew morning prayer went something like this: "I thank you Lord that I am not a slave, that I am not a Gentile, and that I am not a woman." Once again, we see Paul deferring to Christ in Galatians 3: "So there is no difference between Jews and Gentiles, between slaves and free men, between men and women; you are all one in union with Christ Jesus."

Thus we are called, by God, to follow his instructions regarding marital commitment. Overhear a conversation then, if you have ears: A kindergarten teacher friend of mine told me something very profound about the meaning of Jesus' words, "I assure you that whoever does not receive the kingdom of God like a child will never enter it."

She told me that her little five-year-old children come to kindergarten in September totally unfocused and undisciplined. They come not really able to receive anything because their listening skills and their ability to follow directions are as yet undeveloped and untrained. They lack proper self-discipline.

My friend gave me one example, of many she could have given me, of how the young students' listening skills and the discipline of following directions are developed in the life of a little five-year-old kindergarten student.

My friend explained that during daily snack time all of the students get a little carton of milk with a straw. At the beginning of the year she asks her students to listen and follow directions very carefully.

My teacher friend then says to her students, "Now boys and girls, please watch me and do exactly what I tell you to do. First of all, open your milk carton like this (she shows the students how to open milk carton). Now, take the paper wrapper off of your straw (she takes paper wrapper off her straw). Now put the straw into your carton of milk just like I am doing. Now, boys and girls, this is very important. Close the opening in the milk carton back around your straw so that if you accidentally spill your milk you will not lose very much on the table."

My teacher friend goes over these instructions several times with her children to make absolutely sure that everyone understands exactly what they are supposed to do. And she tells me that there are major milk spills until about Thanksgiving time. Milk spills because the children have listening and discipline lapses. They are, after all, only children.

Hence, Jesus does not mean childlike literally. What Jesus means is that if a leader or teacher has your best interest and welfare in mind; that is, if a leader is purely benign, like Jesus, one should follow that leader or teacher literally. One should listen to and follow the directions of that benign leader or teacher, exactly.

There is a warning here also. It would logically follow that one should not follow or listen to a supposed leader or teacher who is out to dictate and dominate in a manipulative fashion.

So when Jesus said to his followers, "You have to be like these children if you want to be nourished by the kingdom," he was saying something like "If you want to be nourished by your milk snack, by not spilling and losing your milk, you're going to have to surrender your own judgment long enough to let someone, who is totally benign, teach you the basics." And the same holds true with marriage. If you are to learn about the commitment of marriage, you're going to have to surrender your own judgment long enough to let our Lord teach you the basics.

Genuine love is being committed to each other no matter how we might feel about one another at the moment. There are those days when I don't like my wife, and there are many more days when she doesn't like me! Because of something one of us did. But regardless of how we feel emotionally toward each other, we are committed, through Christ's love, to love one another unconditionally. To act lovingly toward each other even when we do not like each other. There are times in the family when there is illness, when there has been death, or when spouses have been working long hours apart from one another, when that "romantic feeling" of love disappears. But then there are those moments when spouses do spend time together, vacations, holidays, going out to dinner together, getting away for a weekend alone or spending a quiet day off together, when that "romantic feeling" of love returns once again. Real marital love is being committed, investing in the marital relationship, knowing that the romantic feeling of love will always return. Unfortunately, many married couples invest time and money in everything but their most valuable possession. Our marriage. Our life together. The most valuable gift we can give to our children is a loving and stable marriage. Marriage deserves this kind of commitment. Marriage needs the commitment of love to hold it together.

Spectators Or Sentinels?

Arthur H. Kolsti

Ordinary Time 28
Mark 10:17-30

The Running Man

"And as he was setting out on a journey, a man ran up and knelt before him ..." There is an intensity that clings to these introductory words. They suggest a man driven by some urgent need. Who is he? We are given no name. Perhaps that is Mark's way of inviting all of us to identify with him.

The Greek word that Mark chooses to describe him as running is rare in the New Testament. It has an association with athletics and suggests a forerunner followed by other runners. Might this suggest that our anonymous man is a trendy pace setter who is running in the fast lane? We learn from the ensuing dialogue that judged by the measurements prevailing in his culture he can be called a successful person. He is a decent fellow who has sought to obey all the prevailing oughts. We learn also that he is an achiever and an accumulator. He is beginning to look like a Reebok-shod suburban jogger. Suddenly we realize that though separated from him by 2,000 years, we have much in common.

Outwardly there is much about him with which we can identify. Inwardly also there is a kinship. "Good Teacher, what must I do to inherit eternal life?" That is a heavy question. That is a value-loaded question. Questions of meaning and value are beginning to surface in his life. He is running in more ways than one. That road on which he has been running has suddenly turned into I-95 and he cannot find the exit.

155

Or maybe he feels stuck in the clover leaf. Maybe the career race has turned into the rat race. This fellow is caught up in a crisis of meaning. He is no longer sure of the race. He is a metaphor for many of us. In a football game the ball carrier runs for the end zone. But as Tom Wingo broods in *The Prince of Tides*, "But where do we run when there are no crowds, no lights, no end zones?"

That crisis can assault any one of us. None of us are immune. Listen to these words of a nationally-known sportscaster. "I'm near the top of the mountain I saw as a young man. It's mostly salt." That's the meaning crisis. And that crisis is human enough and normal enough. It's quite apt to slip up on you between the ages of 35 to 65. These are years of transition for you. You are well along in your profession and have established a track record. Perhaps you have reached a plateau. Some advancements have passed by you. Younger people are on the scene and you're beginning to feel not quite up to speed. Your children are increasingly less dependent on you and have probably struck out on their own. These are the years when you will probably lose your parents. The thought of death surfaces in a way it never has before and with it thoughts of your own aging and death. And there is so much in our youth idolizing culture that feeds our anxiety about aging.

These are the vulnerable years when value questions emerge. You take a look around, measure the way you have come and all that you have acquired and wonder, "Is this all there is?" You may feel a desperate push to run faster, be pursued by a haunting fear of becoming obsolete or burning out. You may feel an anxious need to keep on looking young. A face lift may impress your friends, but it will not impress a flight of stairs. Do we begin to own our kinship with the running man? Where is the promised quality in my life? I have played by the rules, what is missing?

"You know the commandments," says Jesus and lists them. "I have kept these since my youth," replies the man. He has been running all his life, prodded by all the admonitions of home, church and culture. Brush your teeth and don't forget to floss . . . say your prayers, work hard . . . obey the law . . . get ahead. Our man had lived by all the imperatives imposed upon him from the outside. That is the way we all grow at first, independently of our own decision. Our parents command us, our teachers teach us, our church preaches to us, society imposes its models and definitions upon us. We go along with the stream of influences. But sooner or later we get to the point where we have to do some deciding and choosing on our own. The running man was reaching that point. Mark tells us that Jesus looked at him and loved him. The Lord understood.

"You lack one thing; go, sell what you own, and give the money to the poor, and you will have treasure in heaven; then come, follow me." Saint Francis took these words literally and the world was made brighter by that decision. But we also can remain true to the text by understanding the words this way. Jesus is asking this man and us to cut the nerve of our dependencies. And so often our possessions represent our dependencies. Jesus is asking this man and us to die to attachments that can provide only a temporary meaning for our lives. His challenge is to disentangle ourselves from our possessions. Roberta Flack sings a song with the intriguing title, *Let Pharaoh Go*. There is a reverse thought that grabs you. We think of Pharaoh as the one who can make the decision to keep us or free us. But so often the reverse is true. We do not want to let go of the things that hold us. After all, the things of this world give a certain kind of identity and assurance.

The theme of renunciation emerges in this encounter, a theme familiar throughout the gospels. Renunciation is a form of dying. We Christians tend to think of death and resurrection as experiences at the end of life, not as possibilities in the midst of life. The New Testament proclaims that the life of faith is a rhythm of death and resurrection, or should I not say deaths and resurrections. We have to die to many things during a life time if we are to experience any sort of new possibility.

Think of the role of being a parent. The satisfactions of parenthood are certainly part of our possessions. The role gives both identity and satisfaction that we are needed. But the time comes when our children leave home. That can be a crisis time. Psychologists speak of the empty-nest syndrome. We have to die to this particular role in this particular shape we have known. Children also, if they are to grow, have to die to parental dependencies. We have to die to our vocational role. A friend once made this comment about a lady who seemed so unhappy, "Her problem is that she is the retired chief operator of the Indiana Bell Telephone Company." Finding identity only in terms of our work is common in our culture. Daring the risk to die to old dependencies is what resurrection faith is all about. We have to die to all our dependencies someday.

Mark tells us that when the running man heard the challenge of Jesus "he was shocked and went away grieving for he had many possessions." Really, his things had him. Jesus did not seem surprised by his departure. He understood how our possessions can bind us. "How hard it will be for those who have wealth to enter the kingdom of God."

Martin E. Marty, writing in *Context,* passes along from Leonard Sweet the story of an Amish man who momentarily stopped his farming to watch a new neighbor move in. Among the many items that came out of the delivery van were a deluxe refrigerator with a built-in ice cube maker, a state-of-the-art stereo system with a compact disc drive, a remote control television with VCR, and a whirlpool hot tub. The following day, the new resident was welcomed by the Amish man and his wife, who brought a gift of homemade muffins and jam. After the usual greeting and cordial conversation, the Amish man concluded with "... and if anything should go wrong with your appliances or equipment, don't hesitate to call me."

"That's very generous of you," the new arrival interrupted.

"No problem," the Amish man replied, "I'll just tell you how to live without them."

Perhaps before any of us are ready to hear Jesus on this subject, we have to reach the point where all our toys begin to fail us and we begin to realize what trifles they are and become open to the love that is life indeed.

Ordinary Time 29
Mark 10:35-45

No Short Cuts To Glory

The disciples were not good listeners. But then, neither are we. Three times on his journey to Jerusalem Jesus told them about the dangers that awaited him and the suffering he anticipated. Three times! And after the third repetition here are James and John waving their resumes in his face and fantasizing about cushy jobs in some glorious kingdom. All the cross talk of Jesus doesn't seem to have registered.

Why not? Could it simply be the all too human propensity not to hear what we do not want to hear? All of us can at times be conveniently deaf. It is common enough for any of us to block out the words we do not want to hear.

Listen! Cross talk is not comfortable for us either. The evidence for saying this lies in our worship attendance records. Which are our two most heavily attended services during the year? We all know they are the Christmas Eve candlelight service and Easter. Which are the two least attended? They are Holy Thursday and Good Friday. In fact, traditional community services across the country have just about gone into eclipse. Doesn't that tell us something? A major weekly television ministry now calls its music prior to Easter not Lenten music, but pre-Easter music. There is something much more preferable to an empty cross garlanded with lilies rather than to a rough crucifix. It is more exhilarating to sing of a Christ throned in heavenly splendor than to ponder the mournful words of the hymn, "Throned Upon the Awful Tree." Thomas 'a Kempis reflected in *The Imitation of Christ*, "Jesus has many lovers of his heavenly kingdom, but few followers of his cross."

Mark hits the church of his and every day right in the solar plexus with his telling of his interchange between Jesus and James and John. Friday comes before Sunday. The crown and the cross are inseparable. The cross illuminates Easter and Easter illuminates the cross. Recognizing the way we bypass the cross in our worship, the latest *Book of Worship* of the United Church of Christ designates the Sunday before Easter as Palm/Passion Sunday. The service opens with a procession recalling Christ's entry into Jerusalem and then turns to focus upon his passion and suffering.

Mark consistently thumps down hard on the 12. He has his reasons. In the church of his day there were a lot of preachers peddling cheap faith; preaching a Jesus without a cross, a divine wonder worker. Then as now there was a ready market for easy promises. During the 1992 political campaign there was a distinct avoidance on the part of candidates during the primaries and later during the campaign to avoid the painful issue of the national deficit. It seems to be a temptation in politics to sugar coat hard truths. There were Jesus traditions circulating in the early church that contained only miracle stories with no mention of the passion. Mark would have none of this marketing of cheap faith that short-circuited the Lord's strenuous call to follow him in his servanthood and obedience.

Believe me, friends, there is more ultimate comfort for you, and care for you, and love for you in the cross talk of Jesus than in facile platitudes or sermons that reduce the teachings of Jesus to a bag of mental tricks to manipulate God or promise neat short cuts to a happy state of mind. The slick talk of carnival pitch-men is directed to people understood by the speakers to be nothing more than easy marks ripe for manipulation. The hard commands of Jesus are directed to people understood by the speaker to be capable of becoming indeed, sons and daughters of God.

And what shall we say of the comfort in his words? Platitudes fall flat spoken in the terminal ward of a hospital. Cheap promises can hardly address the human chaos in so many places on this planet. Sugar-coated answers say nothing to our fears and anxieties. What words can match those of the crucified and risen Lord who comes to us in the name of that costly love that will never let us go and forever calls us to stand with him in the fellowship of his passion.

Jesus gave James and John a cryptic response with some strange questions. You would think they would ask him to explain his words. If they had any questions they did not get a chance to pose them anyway. The other disciples had overheard the conversation and were furious. They had ambitions and fantasies of their own. Any elevation of James and John to high office would not be joyfully celebrated. How green was their envy.

There is an old legend about a holy man who lived in the Egyptian desert. The demons tried their best to seduce him from the path of holiness, but to no avail. All their tricks failed. One day the Devil passed by and noted the consternation of his servants. "Children, what is the problem?" They explained their many failures to succeed in tempting the holy man. "Watch me," said the Devil. He walked up to the holy man and said, "Greetings, friend, have you heard the good news? Your brother has just been appointed bishop of Alexandria." The countenance of the holy man fell as his face turned green with envy.

You can color the other disciples green at the thought of James and John enjoying some preeminence in their midst. Ego tripping and empire building was in the air even among the first followers of Jesus. It was rampant in the church in Mark's day. Read Paul's letter to the church in Corinth if you want a straight forward picture of the ambitions, jealousies and competition running rampant in the church. Let's not pretend we are unfamiliar with such things in the church or in whatever vocational circles we travel. How green can our own envy be when the promotion we believe we deserve goes to another, or someone else is appointed as a full professor, or another gets the nod after the auditions.

All of the gospels make it patently clear that servanthood is the name of our calling and the style of that servanthood is defined by the crucified Lord who came not to be served but to serve. Back in the 1950s a major national magazine did a feature story on *The Ten Greatest Preachers.* The focus was the American scene. Later that feature was followed by another. *The Ten Greatest Churches.* It was immediately apparent that none of the 10 greatest preachers was associated with any of the 10 greatest churches. The author of the report suggested this possibility, "Maybe the great churches had been served by ministers more interested in building a great church rather than a big name."

Mark had church leaders clearly in his sights as he wrote, but the model of servanthood touches all fields of endeavor. The late Senator Fulbright wrote about *The Arrogance of Power* in political life. Voters often take aim at those who in public office seek special percs and privileges. During World War II a number of skilled business people left lucrative positions in industry to serve in Washington for a dollar a year. When their job was done they returned to industry and stayed there. Now such public service is often seen as a stepping stone. One leaves government service and becomes a well-paid consultant to and door-opener for special interests. The past decade of wheelers and dealers has witnessed the eclipse of any idea of servanthood.

But, thanks be, there are still hosts of servants in public and private spheres of life. The real servants may well be anonymous. I have always resented the way people who work for governmental agencies are often snidely referred to as bureaucrats. The pews of our churches are filled with people who work for city, state and federal agencies and loyally plug away to do a fine and decent job for all of us. Their sort of servanthood is certainly part of the work of the church. We could go on to mention folks in so many other vocations and walks of life.

In choosing illustrations for sermons preachers are prone to extol figures like Albert Schweitzer or Mother Theresa. Well, they are shining lights in this century. But as models for us, the average pastor and church member, they can only leave us frustrated. We will not act out our lives on such a stage. But Jesus came to leave behind a community of alternate agendas and values to the acquisitiveness and greed in the world at large. Our little congregations and the small stages on which we will live out our lives are not insignificant to the Lord's enterprise. Among us, things are to be different. It is not out of reach for any of us to reply to the questions of our Lord, "O Master, let me walk with thee, in lowly paths of service free."

Ordinary Time 30
Mark 10:46-52

Seeing And Not Seeing

Think about your eyes. What mysterious, wonderful instruments they are. We who are sighted people do not have to live in a world of perpetual darkness. We do not have to grope, nor be led, nor depend on descriptions given by others. We can see.

But, how well do we see? Do we have eyes that sometimes see not? I propose a brief exercise. Here are some familiar objects. You have seen them before. They are playing cards. These are face cards. How many times in your life have you seen cards like these and played with them? When we were children we built card houses with them. We played games like Slap Jack and Fish or learned to do tricks with cards. Growing up we learned to pass time playing solitaire and enjoyed games like bridge, whist, gin, cribbage and hearts. How many times have you seen a king, queen or jack? How many times have you looked at the face cards in a game of bridge? You know what a king looks like, or a queen or a jack. They are a familiar part of your visual experience.

But how sharply, clearly, fully have you seen them? Of the four kings which is the only one in profile? Of the four queens, which one holds the scepter? Does every queen hold a flower? Does every jack have a moustache? Which jack carries a leaf in his hand and which has a leaf in his hat? Which king holds an axe instead of a sword?

Tradition says the king of spades represents King David. The lion on his vest could well represent the Lion of Judah. The king of clubs is said to represent Alexander the Great who wept because there were no more worlds for him to conquer. There is an orb, the symbol of the world, in his hands. The king of hearts is reputed to be Charlemagne, the first emperor of the Holy Roman Empire. There are crosses on his stole. The king of diamonds who holds the battle axe is said to be Julius Caesar.

Please understand that I am not trying to show off a lot of knowledge about playing cards. I have always been blind to these details until they were pointed out to me. In a hundred games I have seen the faces without seeing them. Ask if I knew what kings, queens and jacks really look like and I'd answer a confident "Certainly." Is it possible to think you see and not see, at least not everything there is to see?

Seeing and not seeing, this is the over-arching theme of the section of Mark's gospel that records the journey of Jesus from Caesarea Philippi to Jerusalem. This section begins in chapter eight at verse 22 with the healing of a blind man and ends with the incident involving Blind Bartimaeus. The section is prefaced by the questions Jesus posed to his disciples, "Do you have eyes and fail to see? Do you have ears and fail to hear?" (Mark 8:18)

It is during this journey that Jesus thrice tells the disciples about the suffering that awaits him in Jerusalem. His cross talk falls upon deaf ears. Visions of courtly splendor fill their eyes. They jockey for position in the coming kingdom and wrangle among themselves as to who shall be the greatest among them. They do not see the glory of Jesus hidden in his servanthood. Remember that blindness is biblical metaphor for spiritual blindness.

Jesus is accompanied by insiders who do not see. He encounters two outsiders who do see. One of them is named Bartimaeus. Dwell for a moment on this encounter. Bartimaeus sits by the roadside begging. Hearing that the Messiah is approaching he shouts out, "Jesus, Son of David, have mercy on me!" Well might he so cry out in fear and trembling. He is blind. The prevailing dogma taught that the blind were blind because of sin, moral blight. The approach of a military messiah could well fill him with terror. The expected Son of David-type messiah would enforce the dogmas of Israel and those whom those dogmas define as morally unfit would have a hard time indeed. That is how Bartimaeus perceived Jesus, as the warrior Messiah. At this point he is just like the other disciples, blind to the meaning of Jesus, locked in a vision of messiahship forged by a culture preoccupied by power and prestige.

Some of those around Jesus tried to hush Bartimaeus up. Roman ears might be listening and zealots in the crowd would be edgy about that. "Many sternly ordered him to be quiet." I hear someone saying, "Shut your mouth or we will shut it for you." Jesus stopped and told his disciples to call the blind man. Was Jesus taking Bartimaeus into protective custody? This is a distinct possibility. Bartimaeus was a social nobody and some zealot could have roughed him up or worse in an attempt to silence him. Fanaticism always hovered on the edges of the crowds around Jesus. Some in the crowd sense that Bartimaeus is getting a break, "Take heart; get up, he is calling you."

The call of Jesus triggers Bartimaeus into immediate action. He flings off his cloak, springs up and comes to Jesus. In response to the Lord's question, he asks that he might see again and Jesus restores his sight. James and John, the insiders, asked for chief seats in the kingdom to come and were turned down. The outsider asks for sight and gets his request.

But he sees something more than faces, forms, objects. He sees Jesus. He perceives what it really means to be a Son of David. He sees what the 12 fail to see. He glimpses the true glory hidden in the cross bearer, a glory to which we are so often blind in the acquisitive society. Bartimaeus perceives a love that gives and in the act of giving makes no demand yet mysteriously compels a freely given response. Note that Jesus told Bartimaeus to go. He does not go, he followed Jesus on the way. The Greek word translated *way* suggests much more than a spatial locating of Bartimaeus. He is with Jesus in the life way of the cross. It is not just his feet that are moving. His heart, mind and will are with Jesus in the service of a new kind of kingdom. This is discipleship.

So Jesus goes on his way to Jerusalem accompanied by sighted disciples who do not see and a sightless man who does see. That same theme crops up in Shakespeare's play *King Lear*. The Earl of Gloster whose eyes were brutally torn from his head shares the suffering of Lear and sees more than the sighted who are blinded by their own ambition and rage. Is there anything really strange about this theme of seeing and not seeing?

Return to the exercise with the face cards. How can one play cards many times through the years, see the face cards and yet not see them? One thing we want to do whenever we play cards is win. That is our agenda. Our attention rivets on one thing, the value of the cards to us. Our concern is with what the cards are worth to us, not with what they look like. Is that a parable of life? Can our vision of God, of the world, of the people around us be impaired by something within? Can we see people in general without ever seeing them in particular and noting that one walks with a limp, another has a tic, another looks worried or depressed? Can a man look at his wife across the breakfast table and not really see her because his head is elsewhere? Can a wife see a husband without really seeing in him what others see? A certain man was receiving an award for brilliant scientific achievement. During the award ceremony his wife commented to the person beside her, "If they had seen George shaving every morning for 25 years, they wouldn't think he is so great." Or as with cards, can our agendas blur our vision? Were the disciples blinded by their own fantasies of glory?

What we see or do not see has a way of getting all mixed up by self interest. In August of 1914 when the German armies swept across Belgium and descended on France, the people of England began to entertain the dreadful realization that the enemy was winning the war. Searching for hope they seized upon a tale that became a national illusion. On August 27th a 17-hour delay in the Liverpool to London railway service inspired a rumor that all available trains were being used to transport Russian troops who had landed in Scotland on their way to reenforce the allies on the continent. They had come from Archangel and were on their way to channel ports. Phantoms were seen everywhere. Strange uniforms were seen in passing troop trains. Ten thousand Russians were reported seen in London marching to Victoria station. Sir Stuart Coats of Aberdeen wrote his brother-in-law in America that 125,000 Cossacks had marched across his estate in Perthshire. An English army officer assured friends he had seen 70,000 Russians passing through England. So it went, seeing that was not seeing.

Just as there is a seeing that is not seeing so there is a blindness that masquerades as seeing. How much evil has been inflicted in history by leaders who say, "We see ... we know ... we see the light at the end of the tunnel?" Could Bartimaeus be us letting others define for us the shape of events around us? Even letting others define for us the truth about ourselves? Could Bartimaeus be representative of all for whom Christ came to give new sight? One way to talk about the opening of eyes is to talk about the emergence of a new consciousness. The civil rights movement in our nation coincided with a new visual judgment, black is beautiful. Certainly Bartimaeus through the love that embraced him suddenly saw himself as much more than a social nobody.

This blind man is you and I in our darkness and even in our self despair. He is you and I as disciples who like James and John let our vision be taken captive by the culture of money and power around us and confuse glamour with glory. But listen, a man has passed our way. A light has shone in our darkness. Return once more to the illustration of the playing cards. Only this time think of the human face of God in history, Jesus Christ. Have we really seen him? You have been to church hundreds of times, gone through many Lents and Easters. Have you heard all there is to hear, seen all there is to see? Maybe you and I are so familiar with this old story that we have missed all the radical details of this love that comes to seek us out and open our eyes to an alternate style of living in that kingdom whose priorities and values are fashioned by a crucified Lord.

Ordinary Time 31
Mark 12:28-34

Less Important Does Not Mean Unimportant

This meeting between Jesus and the unnamed scribe recounted in the gospel reading for today catches our attention because it is such a cordial encounter. We come across it in a section of Mark's gospel marked by controversy and the exchange of harsh words between Jesus and his opponents. Jesus has cleansed the temple and denounced the priests and scribes triggering murderous thoughts in their hearts. He further incites animosity with the parable of the wicked vinedressers. His authority is challenged and he is then baited with trick questions. It is just after Jesus blows his top at some Sadducees who had asked a coarse and mocking question that the unnamed scribe who had been listening to the argumentation comes forward with a serious and thoughtful question that goes right to the heart of matters. "Which commandment is first of all?"

This is an important question politely posed. Review the exchange. Jesus answers with the credo of Israel, "The first is this, 'Hear, O Israel: The Lord our God, the Lord is one; you shall love the Lord your God with all your heart, and with all your soul, and with all your mind, and with all your strength.' The second is this, 'You shall love your neighbor as yourself.' There is no other commandment greater than these." No teacher in Judaism had yet linked love of God and neighbor together in such a serious way. Love is the essence of religious living. The scribe agrees with Jesus, "You are right, Teacher; ... 'to love him with all the heart, and with all the understanding, and with all the strength,' and 'to love one's neighbor as oneself,' — this is much more important than all whole burnt offerings and sacrifices."

This was a new experience for Jesus, to receive a professional compliment. He judges the scribe's answer to be wise indeed. This scribe is an interesting fellow, a thinker. Jesus closes the interview with an enigmatic comment, "You are not far from the kingdom of God." Just what that means is far from certain. The word far can be interpreted literally or figuratively. It can mean that the scribe is not far in terms of his spiritual distance from God or it can mean he is standing right near the kingdom present in the words and actions of Jesus. Jesus just leaves the comment hanging in the air as if inviting or anticipating some future response.

Do you suppose the scribe ever became a disciple of Jesus at some future time? We are so used to thinking of the scribes as opponents of Jesus that we can tend to think of them as the bad guys. They were a mixed group of highly trained teachers who functioned as the custodians of the juridical and theological heritage of Israel. Most of them lived on subsidies from pupils or patrons just as Jesus was subsidized by the wealthy Joanna among others. Only the temple scribes were paid out of the temple treasury. Some were ambitious, some covetous, some inadequate, but the majority pursued their ministries faithfully. They were a mix just like the clergy in any age.

It just could be that this scribe was open to giving Jesus a fuller hearing. Something touched him in the conversation. We know that some later disciples came from the ranks of the pharisaic scribes. The Apostle Paul and his companion Barnabas, the Levite, are notable examples. The organization of Matthew's teaching and traveling pastors certainly resembles a school of scribal teachers.

Of course this scribe wasn't ready to make a big leap. Many of us have difficulties making a full leap of faith. We all have questions. Let our scribe be an example. Grab onto Jesus at whatever point you can and keep on working it out in your own mind. And keep on asking questions. This was not a trick question posed to Jesus. It was genuine and serious. The scribe was open to give a thoughtful ear to what Jesus had to say. Isn't this the basis of any sort of civil discourse, openness to dialogue in the midst of disagreement? Such openness is in danger of going into eclipse today. Too many adhere to fixed ideological positions. Extremists on all sides of some of the burning public issues shout at each other and hurl invectives. Trashing those who disagree substitutes for the thoughtful facing of real issues in much political discourse.

Jesus and the scribe could agree on the priority of loving God and neighbor. There was much more to discuss. What does it mean to love God and who is the neighbor? Why did Jesus just terminate the conversation with that enigmatic comment? "You are not far from the kingdom of God." One answer as good as any is to say that there are some things that cannot be fully explained by words alone. Someone once asked the noted ballerina, Pavlova, what she meant by a certain dance. She answered, "If I could explain it, I would not have to dance it." We know that Jesus had already decided that he would have to dance it out come what may. Remember that the rejection of Jesus was also a rejection of all those to whom he ministered. Through his own ministry he had redefined love as active caring and crashed through every ethnic, cultic and gender barrier that separated people. He knocked down all the litmus tests set down by piety to indicate who was in and who was out. The crucifixion was the human "No!" to the lived out answers of Jesus. The resurrection was the Divine "Yes!"

But we are not quite through with this interchange between Jesus and the scribe. Both Matthew and Luke record it, but Mark's version carries a subtle twist. Recall the scribe's response to the answer of Jesus. "And to love him with all the heart, and with all the understanding, and with all the strength, and to love one's neighbor as oneself — this is much more important than all whole burnt offerings and sacrifices." Jesus accepted this as a wise answer. The words of the prophet Hosea ring in this answer. "For I desire steadfast love and not sacrifice, the knowledge of God rather than burnt offerings."

What do these words tell us? Simply this, living for God and neighbor in the world is more important than what we do inside the church building. Or phrase it another way, the work of the church is more important than church work. The great issues of love and justice take priority over ritual and housekeeping. The great flaw of the devout legalists in the time of Jesus was that they tended to major in minors. That became a problem in the early church also when some preachers wanted to reintroduce a host of cultic requirements into the Christian life. Perhaps Mark reported this conversation just the way he did to remind the members of his community of the great priorities.

Back in the decade of the '50s Gibson Winter wrote a book titled *The Babylonian Captivity of the Church.* He argued that Protestants tended to substitute chores inside the church building for the greater service to God in the world. That tendency still persists. During the '60s the great issues of social justice surfaced in our society with a corresponding rejection on the part of many of the institutional life of the church. Some proclaimed the demise of the local parish. Attendance at chapel services declined in many seminaries. Preaching went out of fashion for a while. The world not the church institution was where the action was. Then came the '70s and '80s and many turned inward and we Christians began to do our Jesus thing inside the church while outside the world went its wild way.

Anyway, here we are moving into the '90s. Yes, the prophets of the '60s were correct. The great issues of love and justice in the world have their unique priority. The great commandment is the most important, what goes on inside the church is less important. Jesus did not challenge the scribes on this. But mark this, being less important does not mean unimportant. If the Christian presence is to be visible and ongoing that requires institutionalization and that means chores and tasks that have to be done. As for "whole burnt offerings and sacrifices," ritual and worship in our lingo, they are not unimportant. John Calvin referred to the regular and disciplined worship services of the church as given by God "as aids to our infirmity."

Think of the making of a marriage. Love is the priority. But what renews love? Fidelity renews love. Countless little remembrances renew love. The celebration of special days like anniversaries renews love. These little rituals renew and sustain the larger relationship. So it is with ritual and worship in the church. These are not the ends of our obedience. Their important function is to nourish us for the ministry of love and justice in the world at large.

Ordinary Time 32
Mark 12:38-44

Dwarfed
By Comparison

Mark is fond of drawing comparisons as he tells the story of Jesus. He does just that in the two deliberately framed scenes presented in our gospel lesson. The poor, vulnerable widow stands over against the learned scribes and the ostentatious rich. What a contrast, the public and financial somebodies and the welfare recipient. Think first of the contrast between the scribes and the widow, the teachers and the taught, the learned theologians and the simple devout believer.

A word about the scribes is in order. They were the brains of the religious community. They were the rigorously and highly trained custodians of the theological and juridical traditions of Israel. Mark overdraws their picture here in order to score by excess. They were as mixed a group as any group of clergy in any time. Many lived on the edge of poverty and yet carried out faithful teaching ministries supported only by subsidies from those they tutored or income from self employment as an artisan. The Apostle Paul who came from scribal ranks was a tent maker. Of course, many were tempted to covet public recognition and to sponge off of the devout who could ill afford such exploitation. But then that sort of hankering after chief seats was going on among the 12 disciples of Jesus and avarice was not unknown in the early church among those leaders Paul called "peddlers of the Word of God." We have examples of that on the religious scene today. There are clerical leaders who covet access to power and love the chief seats at political conventions. We too can get enamored of titles and testimonials.

The story is told of a new pastor in the community who placed a call to the pastor of a neighboring church. "Is Mr. Brown there?" he asked the secretary. A voice oozing affection replied, "No, DOCTOR Brown is not here, do you care to leave a message?" "Yes," said the pastor, "tell him BACHELOR Smith called." While Mark in his way of telling the story had the clergy of his and every day in mind let's include the unordained within the target area. The clergy have no corner on sashaying around. An associate pastor at Riverside Church during the days of Harry Emerson Fosdick recalled a Sunday morning incident when the sanctuary was quite full. Mr. Rockefeller arrived a bit late for the service and seeing the full sanctuary, said to the usher, "Don't bother to find me a seat, I'll just sneak up into the balcony." A huffy worshiper who had just arrived and overheard that exchange snapped at the usher, "You may find me a seat in the sanctuary. I am not the balcony type."

The poor widow in the temple stands there as the model of devout Jewish piety. And there is a comment by the late Swiss theologian, Emil Brunner, that sums up this contrast between scribes and widow, the teachers and the taught. "Greater faith can dwell in the heart of a devout peasant than in the head of the most learned theologian."

Enough said? Well, enough has been said to bring us all down to size. But a warning cries out to be inserted here. There is a sting in this comparison, but it is not to be taken as a charter for anti-intellectualism or theologian bashing in the church. The church needs thoughtful expositors of the scriptures in the classroom and even more crucially in the pulpit. Anne Douglas has written a challenging book, *The Feminization of American Culture*. In the book she has a fascinating and convincing discussion of the effect of the disestablishment of the church in Massachusetts upon Congregational and Unitarian clergy. The clergy experienced a status blow and an identity crisis. They abandoned the one role that was theirs to fill, their role as the teachers and custodians of theological tradition. There has been right through to this time a decline in solid biblical exposition in the preaching ministry. Every decade seems to bring its own fad to the pulpit. During the '70s one pastor asked another, "What are you doing in your church with transactional analysis?" "Not a thing," replied the other, "What are you doing in your church with Matthew, Mark, Luke and John?" Today the fad is the telling of the preacher's personal story as if our little stories could supply the inexhaustible resource of the big story. This is not a clergy issue alone; the whole church is the custodian of the biblical tradition and the expectation of the congregation is involved. Mark's aim is to keep us humble, not to keep us thoughtless.

Scribes are not the only ones who stand in contrast to the widow. The ostentatious wealthy also stand out in comparison to the widow and her pennies. Any number of stewardship homilies have been preached on this scene extolling the widow's offering. The pit into which such sermons can fall is the praise of small gifts. The text has been so romanticized that one ought to avoid it on stewardship Sunday. The figure of the widow does not symbolize today what it did in the days of Jesus. The widow in the New Testament tradition represents the poor and vulnerable because that's what widows were then. They were supported by charity and as women had no role in public life. Today a large share of the wealth of America is in the hands of widows. When stewardship Sunday comes around in late November many of the widows in our congregations are preparing to move to their condos in Florida.

There is a powerful statement about giving here, but it deals with motives. Jesus is watching the ostentatious wealthy put their gifts in the temple treasury. Many of the rich were placing large gifts. It was show time. This was calculated giving to earn brownie points under the law, impress others, gain social recognition, and even to control institutions this way. The devout rich had another alternative. In the temple there was a Chamber of Secrets where the rich could give charitable contributions in secret. This was the way of giving prescribed by Jesus.

Note the rich and poor were in the church together. They were together in the early church. They are together in the church today. The mix was not without its problems. Ostentation and class division posed a severe problem in the congregation at Corinth. In other parts of the church also. Read James' scathing sermon on one congregation's propensity to fawn over the wealthy visitor and ignore the poor newcomer. You'll find the sermon in the second chapter of his epistle. Economic divisions still are a problem mix in the church.

Archie Hargraves, one of the pioneer founders of the East Harlem Protestant Parish, tells of a meeting in the early days of the parish where a group of men from the parish sat down with a group of men from a wealthy suburban church. To begin, the convener suggested each introduce himself and state his work. All of the suburban men had powerful professional and business titles. It was soon noted that the visitors from East Harlem felt dwarfed. The convener suggested that they go around again and each answer the question "Why I am a Christian." The men from East Harlem gave answers that dwarfed their hosts. This is the way our gospel reading gets to the essentials. The gifts of the ostentatious were vastly greater than the two lepta of the widow, but when judged by the measure of her faith and sacrifice, her contribution dwarfed the others. I hear here an imperative that democratizes the church. The importation into the church of the values of the larger culture has no place.

There is a memorable statement by John Knox made during a sermon in St. Giles Church in Edinburgh during the years of his contention with Mary, Queen of Scots. Pointing his finger at the Queen, he declared, "Madame, in the kingdoms of this world you may be a Queen, but in God's kingdom you are just another silly servant." That's all any of us are, just another silly servant.

So here are the contrasts that stare out at us all from the gospel reading. The scribes and the ostentatious rich, the smart set and the jet set, are set over against one vulnerable and poor widow. What a contrast, the big people and the little people, for the widow is one of these. This is a contrast that runs throughout Mark's gospel. In his gospel the little people surface and shine. In Mark's gospel the giants turn into dwarves and the dwarves into giants. The disciples wrangle over chief seats while blind Bartimaeus sees what they do not see. He becomes a giant of the faith while the 12 start looking like the 12 dwarves. The widow dwarfed by privilege and wealth is judged the giant in the faith. As Jesus makes his way to the cross heroism erupts in unexpected persons, Bartimaeus, Simon the Leper, Simon Cyrenean, Joseph from Arimathea, the poor widow, Mary, the mother of James and Joses to name some. They all courageously make some contribution or take some risk on behalf of Jesus. Collectively they make a significant impact. They are little Christ figures and models of discipleship. Meeting them we are ushered into another world of values and measurements. And thinking of the impact of little people think of the grandmothers of the former Soviet Union who have been credited with passing on the Christian faith to children growing up in an officially atheistic state. They are modern day descendants of the widow in the temple.

This story of the widow's offering closes Mark's account of the public ministry of Jesus. Ahead lies the cross. The widow's offering foreshadows Jesus pouring out of his own life on behalf of others. And speaking of contrasts, there is a third group, unseen but present. They are us, the hearers of the story. Over against the widow, how do we measure up, or down?

Ordinary Time 33
Mark 13:24-32

Spectators Or Sentinels?

The gospel reading for this day is bracketed by the command to keep alert, to watch. Suppose I could hang before you a giant photo of the sun peeking over the horizon and asked you to tell me if this were a surprise or a sunset. Could you tell? Only the photographer would know for sure. A sunrise and a sunset are similar in appearance. We can mistake the one for the other.

The fall of Jerusalem and the destruction of the temple had a devastating effect on Jews and Christians alike. It was a sunset. Our gospel lesson speaks to Christians for whom the catastrophic Jewish war marked an end of the world as they had known it. The language of the 13th chapter of Isaiah seemed appropriate. "For the stars of the heavens and their constellations will not give their light; the sun will be dark at its rising, and the moon will not shed its light." (Isaiah 13:10) This is the source of verse 24 in our lesson.

But there is a significant change. The Lord has edited out all references to the destruction of sinners and the fierce anger of God. Instead a new beginning is proclaimed, an ingathering universal in its scope. One age is passing away, another is emerging. Is it a sunset or a sunrise? The old structures crumble, but the gospel goes on, the mission goes on. The green branches signal God's new tomorrow. We can so easily misread the signs in our human experience. When Rome fell to the barbarians a colleague of Saint Augustine bore the awesome news to him. Augustine made the reflective comment, "but the kingdom of God goes on." And so it is that we also go on in the service of that kingdom amid the dislocations of history. And because we know that the switches of history are set on the side of him whose words will never pass away, because in him we have caught a glimpse of God's coming tomorrow, we are called to the sentinel's vocation which is another way to think and speak about the Lord's call to us to join him in the ongoing struggle for justice and peace.

"Watch!" Here is the second of the two grand imperatives uttered by Jesus in this his last discourse with his disciples in Mark's gospel. These commands are spoken not just to the few there and then, but to all of us in the here and now. Jesus makes that abundantly clear. "And what I say to you I say to all: Watch." The New Revised Standard Version translates the command as "keep awake." The word "watch" is still preferable and justified by the Greek usage for the vigilance commanded is that of the sentinel.

Watching is big business today. The need to post sentinels persists in history. Over the last several decades security and surveillance have become growth businesses. Look at the yellow pages of your telephone book and note how many companies provide guard services, burglar alarms or electronic surveillance for homes, shopping malls, business and industry.

Watching is a deterrent. Human and electronic eyes scan the boarding airline passenger and luggage. Spy satellites keep track of what is moving on the face of the earth. Ours is that kind of world. Somebody is always cooking something up. Warning systems are set up to track tornadoes and hurricanes and monitor movements in the earth. It's that kind of planet. Something is always on the way.

Local police departments encourage the formation of neighborhood crime watch networks. Watching helps. When they built the Kennedy Government Center in the city of Boston they erased a good section of Hanover Street in the North End.

I remember the old Hanover Street. It had the look of a tough street when actually it was a safe street. Lots of tenement windows looked out over Hanover Street and numerous immigrant mothers posted themselves at those windows to watch their children playing below. They saw everything. They were sentinels. Theirs was a caring kind of watching that helps us get a hold on this command of Jesus.

In the novel by Andre Schwarz Bart, *The Last of the Just,* there is a scene that involves windows and watching. The locale is Germany in the 1930s. Ernie, a young Jewish lad has been followed into the courtyard of the apartment complex where he lives by a club-swinging pack of Nazi Brown Shirts. Suddenly the Brown Shirts stop their attack and Ernie hears a strange noise above him, jeers. The jeers were directed at the Storm Troopers who were looking up in annoyance. It dawned on Ernie that the windows bothered them. When he looked up he could see the heads of men, women and children in the windows. This was strange since those windows never opened except to throw garbage down on the Jewish residents as they came and went. What had changed? Then way above he caught sight of the familiar face of Herr Julius Kremer, his teacher in the public school. A rebuking finger was pointed at the Brown Shirts and a shrill voice was shouting, "Have you no shame?"

This is the watching of the shepherd. This is watching with emotional and moral content. This is watching that activates conscience and triggers a willed response. This is not "spectatoritis." Someone has coined that word. Spectatoritis is the condition of impassive watching. The spectator is on the side lines, an onlooker. You might say that the spectator is a sort of couch potato inertly watching the human drama with all its joys and pathos and remaining unmoved.

The sentinel is an Advent figure in our Christian tradition. "Watchmen tell us of the night, what its signs of promise are." Lurking behind the figure and the command of Jesus is the prophet Ezekiel who understood his own prophetic role as that of a sentinel. "So you, mortal, I have made a sentinel for the house of Israel." It is an awesome office. It makes the prophet doubly responsible. "If I say to the wicked, 'O wicked ones, you shall surely die,' and you do not speak to warn the wicked to turn from their ways, the wicked shall die in their iniquity, but their blood I will require at your hand." That charge makes the sentinel shiver. But an even more awesome point emerges in the sentinel passages of Ezekiel. (Ezekiel 33:1ff) The greatest danger Israel faces comes from God himself. This is a staggering thought. God is the great danger. There is such a thing as judgment. Human decisions and actions bear consequences for good or ill. Individual and collective moral accountability is in the air. The prophet is impelled to be more than a spectator in the human drama.

One way to sharpen and illustrate to sentinel vocation in contemporary terms is to speak of a unique breed who have emerged in our own midst in recent years. They are called "whistle-blowers." Not too long ago they held a convention in Washington where a number of them spoke to a large audience. They are a varied group of people who in the course of their jobs watch certain things take place and were impelled by conscience to speak out.

There were former CIA people like John Stockwell who spoke out in his book, *In Search of Enemies*. One is a Chicago policeman who founded the Afro American Patrolmen's League when his superiors ignored his reports of unfair police practices in the ghetto. Another is a woman who works in the benefits section of the Veterans Administration. She had been excluded from staff meetings after gathering details on former soldiers contaminated by defoliants used in View Nam. Yet another is a doctor who did a special government study on the effects of working in nuclear plants and found the danger level from radiation 10 times lower than that announced by the government. He was dismissed and ordered to hand over his files. These folk have produced a book, *A Whistleblower's Guide to the Federal Bureaucracy.* They advise watchers how to blow the whistle without losing their cool. The prophet Ezekiel would have been right at home amid the whistleblowers.

There are sentinel organizations that have emerged in recent decades. One thinks of Amnesty International and the eye they keep on human rights violations around the world. There is a similar organization called Africa Watch. We have had occasion to see the sentinel power of the television camera/recorder whether used by a reporter or a citizen. The protesters who filled the streets of Prague as the iron curtain came tumbling down faced the riot police and shouted, "Remember, the world is watching."

There is a sentinel vocation for the church and for individual Christians. It is one of the ways we express care for people. It is a shepherding role. And in expressing that concern specific people and specific situations have to be addressed. It is not enough just to proclaim generalities. That was central in Ezekiel's commission as a sentinel. The whole 13th chapter of Mark's gospel is predicated upon continuing tension between church and the surrounding culture. The retaliation encountered is part of the birth pangs of God's coming new day. The command of Jesus implies a situation of ongoing warfare. To watch is to live faithfully, lovingly, hopefully. The worst thing is to fall asleep. To sleep is to stop praying, to die to God, to become numb to any higher impulse or the prompting of conscience. To sleep is to lay aside the hope of salvation, to put God out of the picture. To sleep is to give in to cynicism and compromise.

The command to watch reaches into the whole spread of life. Someone has said that the most dangerous ism is somnanbulism. There are so many forms of sleep walking: the glazed eyes that never notices one's ideals are being eroded, one's purposes being eroded, the evils that gain strength.

Ezekiel as a sentinel feared the retribution of God. Such scenes of retribution and Divine vengeance are absent from these words of Jesus in Mark. Instead we have a vision of the new day of God's making. In Jesus of Nazareth, our crucified and risen Lord, we have caught a glimpse of the new world order. It will be a day of ingathering and embracing and new beginning. It is that vision we are called to serve in the here and now.

The late J. Wallace Hamilton was one of this century's finest preachers. He compared the situation of the disciple between the times to that of the Connecticut Yankee who had an accident and woke up in the ancient court of King Arthur. The story of course was told by Mark Twain, *A Connecticut Yankee in King Arthur's Court.* As he began to explore his new surroundings this man from the future kept bumping into practices obsolete in his own century. He set about trying to shape things in terms of the future. That is our situation as Christians. We have seen the future in the words, life and actions of Jesus. We have glimpsed nothing less than the agenda of God himself present on our earth. In the crucified and risen Lord we behold the first flashes of love's far ranging victory on the horizon of history. We are sustained by hope as in the here and now we live as the sentinels and servants of that victory that shall surely come in God's own good time.

All Saints' Sunday
Matthew 5:1-12

It's Time
To Rediscover
The Beatitudes

The committee responsible for the wording of the New Revised Standard Version did not replace the familiar word blessed in the Beatitudes with the word happy as has been done in some translations. They preserved an important meaning. The Greek word so translated blessed did bear the meaning of happiness in the wider Greek speaking world. That happiness was defined as a life beyond care, labor and death. A model of such happiness was the life of the gods on Mount Olympus who lived beyond the hassles of everyday mortal life. It became an everyday term that could also mean simply rich. The wealthy who had the means to live without economic anxieties of lesser folk were described as happy. That meaning is not unknown among us. That television program so representative of the decade of the '80s, *The Lifestyles of the Rich and Famous,* takes us right back to the emulation of the gods by the ancient Greeks.

Webster's dictionary defines the word beatitude as "a state of utmost bliss." Do you suppose that is what Jesus had in mind? There is a delightful English comedy series on public television titled, *Waiting for God.* The locale is a retirement home for the elderly. Central to the story is a fiesty, irreverent and unconventional resident who is forever colliding with the staff. The social director is a benign lady with a perpetual smile, a cross hanging around her neck and a verbal fund of religious platitudes. One day the fiesty resident snaps at her, "Oh, stop it, you look like the Mona Lisa on Valium." It is difficult to imagine that Jesus intended to send out into the world a stream of followers wearing smile buttons. Preachers are tempted to present him as a dispenser of mental tricks for attitude adjustment.

The blessings of Jesus do not focus on the external circumstances of the person, but on inner moral and spiritual content. Some redefining is going on here. When we look at those who are called blessed we realize that something radical is afoot here. The blessed are not those the world would call blessed. In terms of what the world would call happiness, Peter, James, John and Andrew were a lot better off in many ways before they encountered Jesus. Economically, for one thing. The fishing industry in first century Palestine was a prosperous enterprise. James and John were doing quite well for Mark tells us that when they met Jesus they left the hired hands in charge of the boats. (Mark 1:20) They were employers. I bet their fish were turning up in all the upscale delis of Jerusalem. Levi, the tax collector turned disciple, had a comfortable position and enough means to throw a big dinner for Jesus in his own home. (Mark 2:15) They were doing quite well before Jesus came along to enlist them in what was destined to become a high risk enterprise in which some of them would even lose their lives. Out of memory comes a line from a hymn, "The peace of God, it is no peace, but strife closed in the sod."

No, this is no guru dispensing mental keys to happiness and healthier attitudes. This is a commander reassuring his troops and pointing them to the victory beyond many a losing battle. This is the risen Lord preparing his church to live, pray and labor for the kingdom in a world where the score will always seem to be Christians 6, Lions 70. We are on the mountain here. The story of Jesus as told by Matthew moves from mountain to mountain. From the mount of temptation to the mount of mobilization and teaching, to the mount of healing, to the mount from whence Jesus comes to deliver his church, to the mount of transfigured seeing, to the mount of the great commission. The mountain is the place of revelation, instruction, command, ordination and assurance. Trace the path of Jesus through Matthew's gospel from mountain to mountain. It is fascinating. And, of course, these mountains point back to Mount Sinai where God spoke to Moses and through him addressed Israel. Some weighty things are being said here through the artistry of Matthew about the one who speaks and blesses. Here is one greater than Moses to whom all authority in heaven and on earth has been given.

And right here the phrase often translated "Happy are you" breaks down and proves inadequate. Jesus is after all giving a blessing and in the faith tradition of Israel a blessing is something special. A blessing conveys the soul force of the giver. A blessing carries an assurance and a guarantee, especially the blessing of God. Go back to the book with that distressing name, Numbers, and read the story of Balaam who was hired by Balak to curse the Israelites. "You shall not curse the people, for they are blessed." Three times God cancels the human curse Balaam would utter and turns it into a blessing. When we read this old story we cannot help but see in it a foreshadowing of the Divine reversal of the human curse of the cross and the reassertion of the blessing of God. "And remember, I am with you always, to the end of the age." The Beatitudes point beyond the present to love's far ranging victory, but they do not ignore the present. Here are the promises that sustain the blessed in the worst of times, in seeming defeat, in many a dark night of the soul. When Lattimore and Gridley were burned at the stake for their non-conformist ways, Lattimore shouted to Gridley, "Be strong, Master Gridley, and play the man. We shall this day light such a fire in England that by God's grace shall never be put out."

With a renewed appreciation of the forcefulness of that word "Blessed," let's take a brief glimpse at a few of the beatitudes. Take the first one. "Blessed are the poor in spirit, for theirs is the kingdom of heaven." Who are the poor? The poor in the gospels include not only the poverty stricken, but all judged by a harsh and ruling piety to be beyond the pale of respectability and the approval of God. The blessing of Jesus signals that the switches of history are set on the side of those who, as he did, turn the situations of human pain, suffering, and alienation into occasions for healing, mercy and reconciliation. To the beatitude as reported by Luke, Matthew makes a slight change, "poor in spirit." We want to remember that Matthew's congregation is removed in time from this group around Jesus. They are not so poor any more. In fact, all the evidence suggests a prosperous, urban congregation. How might we interpret this beatitude to such a congregation? What does it mean to be poor in spirit? I suggest this. To be poor in spirit is to stay connected to the pain of all our brothers and sisters in this world. When we become a community of the comfortable and indifferent, we will have little relevance to the kingdom.

"Blessed are the meek, for they will inherit the earth." Who are the meek? They are the oppressed who are excluded from the mainstream, the people without clout.

They are not silent door mats. They may speak up. They may organize and knock on the doors of power and privilege. But, I think here of the comment of a United Methodist Bishop. "It is true, the meek will inherit the earth. The problem is how to keep them meek once that has happened." I think here of a congregation in colonial Massachusetts. These folk had their eyes on some land owned by the Indians. The following entry was found in the minutes of a meeting they held to decide if they should claim that land. "Voted, the earth is the Lord's. Voted, the saints shall inherit the earth. Voted, we are the saints." In this century we have seen the oppressed assume power and become themselves arrogant and bloody tyrants. We have also witnessed how this arrogance can bring its own unique doom.

The folk in that parish in Massachusetts singled out only one beatitude. They should have gone further and pondered "Blessed are the pure in heart." The late Emil Brunner commented that the church is called "The Church Militant not only because she is in confrontation with the world, but because each Christian is called to an inner struggle of the soul. In instructing his church, Jesus is not setting up an us versus them group. The evils in the world do not exist somewhere else in someone else. They exist also in us. "Only in humility, charity and purity can we be prepared to receive the grace of God without which human operations are vain." T.S. Eliot said that.

That suffices for now. The aim of this homily was to help us all rediscover the Beatitudes for ourselves and the radical way they turn our cultural values upside down. The ancient Greeks called the person rich in things blessed. We still do. The Beatitudes point us to that inner wealth that constitutes true blessedness. Philip Yancy, a columnist, cited in a recent column the people in his own life who manifested great wisdom. Among them was included a patient at a leprosarium in India, a civil rights leader who worked out his theology in a jail cell, a mother who lost two children to cystic fibrosis, a priest who works in a home for the disabled, and a minister turned innkeeper for the homeless. His concluding comment will be of interest to us. "At one point in my life I pitied such people. Then I came to admire them. And now I envy them. They help me understand the Beatitudes which jar me because I now recognize in them a richness that unmasks my own poverty."

If you covet the phony happiness of the world, read the glossy magazines. If you covet blessedness, heed the Lord who speaks from the mountain and follow him.

Christ The King
John 18:33-37

Where Do We Stand?

On the last Sunday of the church year, who would expect to come face to face with Pontius Pilate? Doesn't his memory belong back in the Lenten season? What on earth is he doing here at the end of November? The answer is that this last Sunday of the church year has traditionally been called The Feast of Christ the King and the kingship of Christ is John's major theme in the 18th and 19th chapters of his gospel. Pilate ironically paid Jesus the highest tribute by placing on the cross an inscription written in three languages, Jesus of Nazareth, the King of the Jews. In the act of defiance directed at the chief priests Pilate unwittingly extended the royalty of Jesus far beyond the borders of Judea.

It is Pilate that we are going to focus in on this morning. John has woven into his telling of the trial and passion of Jesus a profound study of Pilate. Since Pilate is prominent in our gospel reading, it is quite appropriate to take a close look at him. And surprise, surprise, as we do this each one of us will find the royal claim of Jesus intruding into our conscience, the place where he really seeks enthronement.

What we know about Pilate can be quickly summed up. He was the Roman Procurator of the imperial province of Judea from 26 to 36 A.D. The volatile Middle East has never been an easy place to be assigned. Keeping order required a strong hand. Pilate showed he had such a hand when he spilled the blood of some Galilean zealots. Another time he took funds from the temple treasury to build a new aqueduct for Jerusalem. The act provoked a public uproar and Pilate had to clear the streets by sending out troops with cudgels to disperse the crowds by cracking heads. On another occasion he provoked a riot by having his troops parade through Jerusalem bearing the Imperial standards which displayed an image of the emperor. Pilate ought to have known that the display of the image of a man who claimed divinity would provoke Jewish sensitivities. Like all Roman administrators he was impatient with the religious particularities and disputes in this part of the world. It is also reported that he was finally recalled to Rome to answer for his mistaken slaughter of some Samaritans, a mistake that led to his banishment. Another report has it that he retired to Vienne in Gaul. He just seems to disappear into history. We do know that he was married and his wife, Procula, was with him in Jerusalem. Matthew reports that she had a bad dream and warned him to do nothing to the innocent Jesus.

Suffice it to say that Pilate had a tough job in a complicated part of the world. Given the way some of our own leaders and appointees have blundered in various places on this globe we can refrain from passing judgment on Pilate as the representative of Imperial Rome. In the gospels Pilate is not presented as a brutish person. John, as a matter of fact, gives us a rather human portrait of the man. He really did not want to be involved in a Jewish religious quarrel or even a criminal case that they could handle by their own laws. When the captors of Jesus mentioned that they desired the death penalty he had to interrogate Jesus.

"Are you the King of the Jews?" He had to have an answer to that question. Jesus puts him off balance. "Do you ask this on your own, or did others tell you about me?" Jesus suddenly becomes the interrogator. He has confronted Pilate with the responsibility of making up his own mind. He cleverly implies that Pilate might have some interest in him. Hear

Pilate's reply. "I am not a Jew, am I?" Does this mask a deeper question, "Are you my King also?" Pilate is inwardly off balance, but he has to determine the reason Jesus has been handed over to him. "What have you done?" Jesus does not answer directly, but speaks of a kingdom not of this world. His is not the way of violence. "So, you are a king?" Jesus reminds Pilate that he is the one who says Jesus is a king. Then Jesus states his mission. "For this I was born, and for this I came into the world, to testify to the truth. Everyone who belongs to the truth listens to my voice." Pilate is rattled. He asks a question. "What is truth?" Was this a cynical reply, or the beginning of interest, or simply a lack of comprehension? At any rate, Pilate does not wait for an answer. This portion of John's narrative ends with a question. It's just left dangling there. Maybe John wants us to reflect on who or what is truth.

As the narrative moves on you will recall how Pilate tried one way after another to release Jesus. Pilate succumbs to pressure until the enemies of Jesus play their trump card, reminding Pilate that Caesar would not want him to tolerate any other authority in Judea. During the Passover that marks their liberation, the enemies of Jesus embrace the Pharaoh, "We have no king but the emperor." In the end, Pilate acted to save his own skin. We are indebted to Raymond Brown for this astute comment on John's portrait of Jesus. "We would look on the Johannine Pilate not as a personification of the State but as another representative of a reaction to Jesus that is neither faith nor rejection. Pilate is typical not of the state that would remain neutral, but of the many honest, well disposed people who would try to adopt a middle position in a struggle that is total."[1]

Soren Kierkegaard called the Word of God a mirror in which we see our own reflection. Well, here we are face to face with Pilate. Or is that our own face staring back at us? Did you know that Pilate was canonized in the Ethiopian Church? There is a tradition that he was a secret Christian. We can doubt that, but there is no doubt that a lot of the folk who would read John's gospel were secret Christians within the establishment who feared public intimidation and so silenced their convictions. Many of those would see mirrored in Pilate their own tragic temporizing and indecision.

How about us? I cannot speak for you, but I know that on many issues I have learned to tolerate a dull ache in the region of conscience. Pilate caved in when his own self interest was at stake. Do we do the same thing in the office, in the ivied halls of academe, in the club, in the community, in the church? "But each day brings its petty dust, our soon filled souls to clog. And we forget because we may, and not because we must."

Suddenly now the focus is not on Pilate, but on us. The framers of our lectionary have done better than they knew. This gospel reading brings the Kingship of Christ to us with uncomfortable questions. Where do we stand in terms of his Royal claim upon us who bear his name? Is he our King? If so, then, "Let every heart prepare him room." He is coming soon. For us, there are still days of grace. Who knows, we may yet make sainthood in someone's calendar.

---

[1]Brown, Raymond E., The Gospel According to John, XIII-XXI. *The Anchor Bible,* Doubleday & Company, Garden City, New York, p. 864.

Thanksgiving Day
Matthew 6:25-33

Good Powers Wonderfully Hidden

Our gospel reading is part of the Sermon on the Mount. It is important to keep that larger setting in mind for these words are directed to disciples and to those who have allowed Jesus to call them to God. Jesus is mobilizing his community for a high risk enterprise. They are to march into history by a different drum beat. "You have heard it said to those of ancient times . . . but I say to you." And what staggering things he said. What anxiety inducing commands. What radical ethical and moral imperatives fell from his lips. Imperatives whose servants a belligerent and alienated human community would resist, resent and fail to understand. No wonder that, as if sensing the way he was raising the anxiety level of his disciples, he speaks to those inner restraints their fears would impose upon them. "Therefore I tell you, do not worry . . ." Those wonderful words of promise that were read to us this morning roll out to all of us would be intentional disciples who share the vulnerability and fragility of the little birds of the air. To all of us who in our search for security clutch to our bosoms those prized securities the world tells us are so necessary; those visible things to which we find it much easier to offer our trust than to a hidden and invisible God.

It is also important for us to remember that these words have been especially arranged by Matthew as Dominical instruction for the itinerant preachers and teachers of his congregation, an affluent community probably centered in the prosperous city of Antioch. Like us, they were removed by time and geography from the earthly Jesus. Like us, they lived in a seductive society, many of whose values were framed by the market place.

So did the original hearers of the Sermon on the Mount. Our images of first century Jerusalem tend to be all stained-glass images woven of piety and prayer. More than prayer was in the air. The Court of Herod set a much envied standard of opulence that invited social imitation. The lifestyles of the rich and famous have always exerted a popular appeal. Merchants thrived selling luxury goods to the nobility and wealthy. Conspicuous consumption and ostentation was rife. There was a great market for ointments and jewelry. Some inventive artisan came up with an expensive hair piece for wealthy ladies, The Golden Jerusalem. It was deemed suitable for Sabbath wear. Speaking of ointments, think of the expensive array of lotions for men and women arrayed in any department store or upscale boutique today. While ordinary priests lived on the edge of poverty, the priestly nobility had much wealth, landed property and controlled the temple treasury.

Several years ago the Rockefeller Foundation undertook a study of education in the United States. The study concluded that the images of the market place were powerful shapers of the values of young people. The dominant human image presented to them was and is that of the consumer. This image, concluded the study, gives an inadequate account of the well springs of human life. Yet the influence is pervasive. Just think, for example, of the medical concern for teenage girls who diet dangerously in obedience to the cultural dictum that slim is beautiful. Or think of young men who will shoot one another in tussles over name brand running shoes.

The late Herbert Gezork, a most inspiring man, who served as president of Andover Newton Theological School once interrupted a lecture he was giving to a class in social ethics to make a profound observation that has proved to be prophetic.

This was in the immediate post World War II years when our nation was mobilizing resources to reconstruct war-damaged Europe and beginning to face the new challenge of Soviet expansionism. He told us to be thankful for this national challenge that would demand some sacrifice. Without it we would face a wave of materialism. He did not anticipate the materialism that even with that challenge would accelerate through the decades of the '50s to '80s. Now the challenge of Soviet expansionism has receded. Within the former Iron Curtain nations there is a pent-up demand for consumer goods. That is understandable. But the warning of Dr. Gezork still stands. Veterans who remember a war-scarred Europe in 1944 and 1945 where scarcity was the rule cannot help but be struck by the way the Western Europe of 1992 is becoming an attractive and prospering bazaar.

This is Thanksgiving Day, above all a time to recognize the Creator and Giver of all things. It is also a time to put things in perspective. It is a time to hear Jesus remind us that the grass withers and the flower fades and we share the condition of the vulnerable and transient birds. It is a time to hear him tell us to seek first the kingdom of God, to renew our understanding of who we are and whose we are. Certainly we give thanks for benefits we enjoy, but is there anything in them that will ultimately sustain and save us?

You can visit a reconstructed Plymouth Village today in Massachusetts. The furniture and dress and homes of the Pilgrim fathers and mothers have been faithfully reproduced. Guides will tell you what they wore, how they farmed, how they made butter. But there is a strange silence about why on earth they set out from Leyden in the first place. The popular answer is that the Pilgrims came here that they might worship God as they pleased. That fits an anything goes individualism, but it is the wrong answer. Get this! The Pilgrims came here that they might worship God in a way they believed was well pleasing to him. These were a people on a high risk journey. These were a people under the imperatives. Scarcity, vulnerability and uncertainty were still the rule on that first

Thanksgiving Day. The sod on the graves of many of their loved ones was still fresh. In the midst of extremity they could yet praise and affirm their trust in God the ultimate source of their security.

The title of this homily was taken from a statement of Dietrich Bonhoeffer written from his Nazi prison cell. "By good powers wonderfully hidden, we await cheerfully, come what may." The words of our gospel reading throb and echo in that statement. The words are worth committing to memory. A word of promise has been given to us that no circumstance can cancel out. We give thanks for what is seen, but things seen are perishable and can let us down. Above all, we give thanks for what is not seen.

The book of the prophet Habakkuk closes with a most unusual paean of praise and thanksgiving.

> *Though the fig tree does not blossom,*
> *and no fruit is on its vines;*
> *though the produce of the olive fails*
> *and the fields yield no food;*
> *though the flock is cut off from the fold*
> *and there is no herd in the stalls,*
> *yet I will rejoice in the Lord;*
> *I will exult in the God of my salvation.*
> *God, the Lord, is my strength;*
> *he makes my feet like the feet of a deer,*
> *and makes me tread upon the heights.*

In the 19th century, William Cowper used these words in his beautiful hymn, "Sometimes A Light Surprises."

> *Though vine nor fig tree neither*
> *Their wonted fruit shall bear,*
> *Though all the field shall wither,*
> *Nor flocks nor herds be there;*
> *Yet God the same abiding,*
> *His praise shall tune my voice,*
> *For while in him confiding*
> *I cannot but rejoice.*

Christian friends, hold on to such words and they will hold onto you.

www.ingramcontent.com/pod-product-compliance
Lightning Source LLC
Chambersburg PA
CBHW070535170426
43200CB00011B/2433